Bobbing for Apples—
With Success!

Practical How-To's for
Congregational Leaders

By Carolyn McBride

LANGMARC PUBLISHING • SAN ANTONIO, TEXAS

Bobbing for Apples—With Success!

Practical How-To's
for Congregational Leaders

By Carolyn Mcbride

Editor: Christy McBride
Cover Artist and Text Illustrator: Patty Cargill
Cover Graphics: Michael Qualben

Copyright © 1995 Carolyn Mcbride
First Printing, 1996
Printed in the United States of America

Library of Congress Cataloging-in-Publication Data in Process

ISBN: 1-880292-09-2

CONTENTS

ACKNOWLEDGMENT

I am deeply grateful to my family for their loving support during the process of writing this book. My husband's wisdom and counsel have been invaluable. I am also grateful to our three daughters, Melissa, Keri, and Christy, for their ongoing encouragement. Christy, especially, has been a companion of the heart, sharing her expertise during the editing phase of the manuscript.

My artist friends, Patty and David Cargill, shared my vision. Patty's delightful illustrations and beautiful cover complemented my text exactly as I had hoped. I extend heartfelt appreciation to those who urged me to write this book and to all my dear Christian friends who labor in the vineyard as fellow workers in the church. To serve the Lord through his church is a high calling!

PREFACE

Remember the special excitement of playing childhood games in the crisp, fall air? In my neighborhood, bobbing for apples was always a favorite. Children knelt around a tub of rippling water, watching apples dance on the surface. With keen anticipation we imagined, each in turn, that we would surely catch a juicy prize. Plunging our faces into the water, we tried and tried to catch the slippery objects in our mouths—and fell back in disappointment when the apples floated beyond our grasp. Frustration wasn't the only result of those attempts, however. Giggles quickly followed as each face emerged dripping wet, but without a prize.

This childhood game provides an interesting analogy for describing ministry efforts in the modern church. Often we are like children bobbing for apples, shifting our attention from one apple to another. Much of our ministry is characterized by random, haphazard efforts. Our dreams, like the shiny apples, often seem to hover just beyond our reach. We miss the mark for lack of strategy. Failure to grasp an apple in childhood play may result in laughter, but failure to achieve our goals in the church only produces disappointment.

The church needs a strategy for accomplishing its ministry goals. It needs to prioritize objectives and develop a clear-cut plan of action for attaining them. How can this be done? Purposeful ministry includes several key elements: a unified view of primary tasks, leadership training, streamlined organizational systems, and annual goals. If we understand the importance of these components and make necessary changes, we will see significant and sustained achievements rather than only occasional success.

Bobbing for Apples—With Success! will help you develop an overall strategy for achieving your goals. This

book provides practical tips to help your church revitalize organizational life so that your ministry can be more
effective. Plan for success. Dynamic ministry is possible.
It is within *your* grasp!

SYSTEM VITALITY
SECTION ONE

CATCHING THE VISION

Church organizations have the potential to transform congregational life. If people have a vision for ministry and enthusiastic leaders, they are usually motivated to commit their time and energy to make dreams become reality. Catching the vision begins when one or several people see a need for change and care enough to seek new directions.

The church has often been lazy in its approach to organization. Few people are eager to risk changing old patterns. Too often we seek change only when we become convinced that it is the only way to avert disaster. A church may have adequate financial resources and capable leaders, but unless the whole environment of organizational work is conducive to progress, its ministry may be ineffective. Leaders may be discouraged and not understand why things aren't happening.

Consider your church's organizational life. Are people excited about what is being accomplished? Are meetings productive? Are programs effective? Perhaps your answers to these questions indicate that change is warranted. If your heart is stirred with excitement as you imagine more dynamic ministry, then you may be the person God has chosen to light the fire of change.

Wisdom dictates that you begin by evaluating the existing situation. Certain aspects of organizational life will emerge as major weaknesses. Section One initiates this process of evaluation and change by providing an overview of all aspects of the organizational system. Practical tips will help both pastors and laypersons identify areas that need improvement so that changes can be made. Sections Two and Three will expand these ideas with step-by-step how-to's for implementing change.

1

The Goal: Vitality

> Congregational vitality exists when there is enthusiasm, commitment, and effective ministry.

Vitality connotes vigor, health, energy, and strength. Just as there are ways to measure individual vitality, there are indicators that help us discern congregational health. Where there is vitality, Christians characteristically care for one another, express joy in worship, demonstrate excitement about ministry, and receive newcomers with warmth and enthusiasm. Thus, even when we first enter a fellowship of believers, we can begin to sense its degree of health.

The vitality of the early Christians excites our imagination. We long for a similar corporate experience of the love and fervor that accompany a dynamic faith. But what produces such vitality? If desire alone guaranteed results, many more churches would be growing and alive.

Church history and our own experience teach us that renewal and vitality are of God, not man. Only the Holy Spirit working in the hearts of believers who are open and teachable can produce new life. When faith ignites, believers are led to greater service and stronger witness. We pray for that to happen.

Church history and our own experience also teach us that people inadvertently create significant hindrances to renewal. Cumbersome, ineffective organizational systems are one such hindrance in the modern church. An organizational system involves all aspects of a congregation's activity—methods for selecting leaders and volunteers, number of committees, use of goals, agendas for meetings, accountability requirements, pastoral involvement, and evaluation procedures. When organizational systems work well, programs are more successful and congregations grow. When organizations bog down, ministry suffers and attendance usually declines. Unfortunately, many congregations ignore signs of difficulty far too long; they operate the same way year after year despite the obvious ineffectiveness of their habits. They are unable or unwilling to initiate creative change.

Organizational effectiveness and spiritual vitality are related but not synonymous. Organizational systems are important because they create the environment of order and efficiency needed to carry out ministry. The mechanics of ministry can either hinder or facilitate a congregation's desire to experience spiritual vitality.

Organizational malaise in a congregation indicates that the quality of corporate life needs attention. Consider your church's organizational life. Would the following signs of malaise apply?

- Few members volunteer to work on committees.
- Leaders experience burnout and discouragement.
- Overlapping duties cause confusion and hurt feelings.

- Committees meet, but nothing is accomplished.
- No one seems to know what anyone else is doing.
- Excitement and sense of mission seem rare.
- The pastor's role is unclear.
- Each year the nominating committee finds it difficult to complete its slate of candidates.
- New ideas are usually rejected for fear of offending members.
- People often become so worn down with church work that their joy in the Lord diminishes.

If such conditions exist in a congregation, there is a need to look at the "how" of corporate life. *How* does the congregation operate? *How* does it manage its affairs?

Many churches today are floundering and adrift. As disillusionment grows, members wistfully long for the good old days, but a return to past patterns would not solve their problems. It is no wiser to ignore modern wisdom regarding leadership and organization than it is to ignore modern technology in the field of medicine. New ways to operate more effectively do exist. Why cling to old ways if they no longer work? If the contemporary church is to move Christians toward renewal, it must become a strong vessel—effective in its organizational structure and clear in its purpose.

Some would argue that the only concern of the church should be spiritual matters. Yes, the church is primarily a spiritual entity, but the way it functions from day to day must be given attention. Finances, programs, facilities, and staff are all aspects of the church that require management. The need for organization became clear in the earliest days of the Church when Stephen and others were chosen to administer food to the needy in order to free the apostles for prayer and teaching (Acts 6). A plan was needed then. A plan is needed today. Organizational vitality is a worthy goal.

The environment for ministry, like the tub used for apples, must be sturdy and appropriate. When it breaks down, leaders need to locate and repair elements which do not work well. Rarely can a single action strengthen a faltering organizational system. Problems usually exist due to a combination of weaknesses. The next five chapters survey the organizational system to help leaders identify trouble spots and develop strategies for change.

Congregational vitality is encouraged and promoted by organizational systems that work. Specific steps can be taken to cure the malaise that results when congregations neglect internal patterns of operation. Organizations can become dynamic channels for ministry rather than roadblocks to vitality.

2

ORGANIZATIONAL KEYS:

PURPOSE, SIMPLICITY, LEADERSHIP

A well-organized church is one that is organized around its purpose and effective in attaining it.

FIRST KEY:

ESTABLISH CLEAR GOALS!

Myth: "Establishing goals is a waste of time. We all know what to do. After all, we've been in the church for years."

Reality: Without a goal to guide our planning, we waste time, often move in nonproductive directions, and lack a means of evaluation.

Maintenance or growth? Congregations tend to continue year after year without a clear sense of direction.

Members operate under the comfortable assumption that they are doing the Lord's work. They make random efforts without any clear goals in mind.

Activity without focus, however, usually results in mediocrity. A congregation without goals may preserve life, but it usually does not move forward; it may exist but have no impact on the community. Such a congregation often has a rather boring corporate life. Members rarely feel excited about ministry because they have no sense of accomplishment or progress. Their lack of enthusiasm discourages others from joining their fellowship.

Many congregations today exist with maintenance ministries. They preserve the status quo and take no risks or initiatives. How can a congregation move from maintenance to growth? The first step is to set clear goals and to pursue them aggressively. Goals help people focus their efforts in order to make significant progress.

Congregations can express their goals on several levels. A vision statement is an overall goal describing the congregation's mission or fundamental purpose. An annual goal sets forth a corporate action step designed to advance ministry in accord with the vision statement. Committee goals are detailed plans to upgrade specific areas of activity.

Step 1: Congregational Vision Statement

A vision statement defines a congregation's own unique calling and response to the Gospel and becomes the foundation for ministry and mission.

Every congregation needs a clear and specific vision statement. Why are we organized as a congregation? What do we want to accomplish? This initial decision precedes all other planning. The focus chosen becomes an umbrella goal designed to last for many years or until circumstances warrant revision. The vision statement should not be buried in an office file. Rather, it should be advertised and promoted as a unifying center of organizational planning.

A vision statement facilitates effective organization in two important ways:

• *A vision statement encourages purposeful activity.* A clear, specific vision statement serves as a guideline for all committees. When construction workers pour concrete sidewalks, they work within preset forms made of wood. The boundaries guide the wet cement. Likewise, when committee members brainstorm to get ideas and plan programs for the year, they must work within larger goals and guidelines. The vision statement provides a standard by which to evaluate all programming ideas. Will our programs help us achieve our primary goal? What purpose do they serve?

• *A vision statement promotes stability.* A church that changes its focus frequently may never achieve significant progress. A vision statement provides continuity through changes in leadership and guides thinking when new programs are under consideration.

Step 2: Congregational Annual Goal

The annual goal is an action step designed to help accomplish the overall mission of the congregation.

Once a vision statement is adopted, the governing body of the congregation targets a specific area of church ministry for emphasis. Leaders then set a goal related to this emphasis; the goal is fairly broad but will become more specific as committees strategize and find ways to accomplish it.

For example, an annual goal for a congregation's commitment to outreach might be, "We want to establish home discussion groups so that members can gain confidence in sharing their faith."

Annual goals are the backbone of congregational planning. They usually relate to program development or personal growth. Sometimes they require financial support. Ideas for goals may originate with members, committees, or with the governing body. The governing body gathers ideas and makes a decision based on how well the goal will help the congregation accomplish its mission.

One goal per year usually works best if leaders wish to galvanize maximum support; an annual goal is broad enough to cover many related specific actions by committees. If a congregation adopts more than one annual goal, progress will probably be more difficult to achieve.

Adopting an annual goal does not mean that all other work ceases so that members can concentrate on the annual goal. It means that while maintaining regular activities, the entire congregation works together to achieve a particular goal that will help members advance their ministry in harmony with the vision statement. Significant progress is much more likely to occur if everyone is aware of the desired outcome and contributes to the effort. The congregation's ongoing ministry tasks will not be neglected in the process.

A clear annual goal for a congregation serves three major purposes:

• *It helps a congregation prioritize ministry efforts.* "What specific step shall we take this year to help us accomplish our mission (vision statement)?"

• *It provides committees with a guideline for planning.* Members of each committee ask, "What can *we* do to help accomplish the congregational goal?" Plans will be made for a specific contribution related to the annual goal. In this way, cooperation among ministry groups also is encouraged.

• *It becomes a tool for evaluation.* Did our activities help us accomplish the annual goal? In other words, the congregation's criteria for success at the end of a year is not how many programs were provided but whether or not these programs led members closer to achieving the congregation's designated goal.

STEP 3: COMMITTEE GOALS

Committee goals are action steps in specific areas of congregational ministry. They are the strategies that translate ideas into actions.

Once the congregation establishes an annual goal for the year, committees enter the picture and begin to consider how each can contribute toward accomplishing the annual goal. As strategies emerge, the workload is shared and implementation begins.

A **vision statement** answers the questions, *What is our primary task?* and *Why are we here?*
The congregation's **annual goal** answers the question, *What action shall we take this year?*
Committee goals answer the question, *How shall we contribute to the action?*

Committees form a congregation's work force. Traditionally, we describe the unique function of each committee in our constitutions. By assigning specific responsibilities to different groups, we avoid overlapping of effort and confusion in planning.

A common flaw in our use of the committee system, however, is that while we identify general responsibilities for each group, we fail to encourage committees to develop specific annual plans. People sometimes assume committee goals are unnecessary. However, two types of goals are vital to success: those related to the congregation's annual goal and those related to ongoing ministry responsibilities.

• *Partnership Goal*—The first obligation of a committee is to adopt a short-term goal related to the congregation's annual emphasis. This can be called a partnership goal; it changes each year in order to conform to the congregation's annual goal. The church as a whole has a big job. The challenge is to see how the job can be broken down into manageable parts so that everyone can carry a share of the load. Work becomes exciting when viewed as a team effort toward a common goal. Basically, this is the concept of "many hands make light the load."

Each committee considers a specific way in which it can help achieve the congregation's goal for the year. What can our committee contribute to accomplish the goal? How can we help?

Suppose the congregation adopts an annual goal related to outreach. How could a property committee, for example, find some way to help with an outreach goal? One possibility would be to direct special attention toward church signs in the community and on highways so that visitors can easily locate the church.

• *Ongoing Ministry Goals*—The second obligation of a committee is to establish goals related to its designated responsibilities. What shall we concentrate on this year?

Activity, in and of itself, is not a desirable goal. A committee or church can have many events and programs but still not accomplish anything that furthers the Kingdom of God. The need, therefore, is to make our activity purposeful.

An educational program, for example, is not successful just because it provides teachers and materials year after year. Leaders should evaluate the effectiveness of those teachers and materials in the light of the congregation's stated purpose. If the learners are not getting excited about their faith, perhaps changes are needed. A stewardship program is not successful just because pledge cards are distributed, offerings are received, and the church remains solvent. If members are not excited in their giving and growing in their generosity, perhaps changes are needed.

Committee members cannot possibly attach equal importance to all of their assigned responsibilities. Therefore, once they understand the scope of their ongoing tasks, they need to establish priorities and set goals accordingly.

SECOND KEY: SIMPLIFY ORGANIZATIONAL STRUCTURES!

Myth: "More is better."

Reality: Less may be more effective.

Many churches today are overorganized. New committees emerge as solutions to whatever needs arise. Frenzied activity in congregations becomes synonymous with faith and vitality. Committee work may even be considered a good strategy for recovering inactive members or integrating new ones. Some people believe that if we can just get a person involved (on a committee), he or she will become an active and excited member of the church. Sometimes, however, the experience of working on a church committee has the opposite result.

> *Consider John:* Baby boomers John and Carol were estranged from the church during their college years and the early years of their marriage. With the birth of their first child, they felt a desire to reconnect. They joined Trinity Church. At first John felt a bit out of place due to his years of absence from worship. He hoped his faith would be rekindled. He wanted to learn, and he also wanted to experience Christian fellowship. Someone asked him to serve on the Property Committee of the church. He was told that serving on a committee was a great way to get to know people and feel a part of the church. He agreed to participate.
>
> In the months that followed, he experienced boring meetings and felt no one was interested in him as a person. People seemed petty at times and certainly

lacking in faith and boldness. Their only guideline seemed to be that they should avoid spending money. John found his ideas were usually ignored.

Judging the congregation by John's committee experience, John and Carol soon began to look elsewhere for a church home.

A congregation should evaluate both the number and effectiveness of its committees. How many committees are there? Are they all necessary? Do they function well? The structure should be streamlined to include only those committees deemed essential. Energy should then be directed toward improving the effectiveness of those groups so that they become exciting, innovative, and dependable ministry teams.

Committees are designed with twin objectives in mind: one is to develop a work force to carry out a congregation's ministry; the other is to provide opportunity for members to use their talents, interests, and experiences to serve God. Committees should facilitate ministry, but if they do not function well, they may actually hinder ministry.

How can that happen? An overorganized church can become competitive internally. After all, the pool of potential volunteers is limited. If too many people are drafted for committees, fewer will be available for other important tasks such as teaching, visiting the sick, singing in choir, and so on. Conservation is always a necessity. The members are a resource that can easily be depleted if leaders compete with each other for success in various programs of the church.

A burgeoning network of committees can also be counterproductive to spiritual vitality. In today's busy world, people make choices. They have limited time and often must choose carefully how that time will be spent. Sometimes harried people choose to do organizational work instead of prayer and study because they feel guilty if they do not serve. Church work should not become a substitute for devotional life; we need to encourage members to set priorities that include spiritual growth.

Churches today have become competitive. Members realize that good programming is essential to growth. By in large, they are willing to volunteer hours of time in committee work because they hope their efforts will contribute to congregational vitality. The excitement of what could be achieved leads them into hours of thinking, phoning, organizing, and doing. The church's obligation is to channel this energy into fruitful avenues and avoid wasting time in unproductive activity. If the overall committee system is streamlined, more people can participate in other aspects of ministry. Those who serve will not become exhausted or discouraged. "Less" is more effective because it reflects good stewardship of members' time, abilities, and resources.

Organizational activity can be improved by using the following guidelines:

• Consolidate committees. Arrange group ministry tasks into a limited number of major categories; as few as possible should be used in order to streamline the structure. These might include worship, education, outreach, congregational life, service, and administration.

• Staff committees with people who have interest, experience, or ability to serve in that particular capacity.

• Limit terms of service for committee members to guard against stagnation or monopoly by a few. A combination of experienced members and new members is desirable.

• Encourage members to limit other church commitments while serving on a standing committee so that they can concentrate maximum effort on that service.

• Stress that committee work involves more than sharing ideas at meetings. Give each member a specific responsibility so that he or she is actively engaged. Be sure that responsibilities are clear and encourage accountability.

THIRD KEY: STRENGTHEN LEADERSHIP!

Myth: "Things will work out. They always do!"

Reality: Careless leadership in a congregation undermines effectiveness. Although random programming successes may occur, overall progress depends on efficient leadership.

Leadership roles in a congregation are of the utmost importance. When leadership is weak, duplication of effort may occur, lack of communication may lead to hurt feelings, committees may become competitive, and a general lack of unity may lead members to conclude that nothing is being accomplished.

If an organizational system is to become more effective, congregations need to evaluate the process they use for selecting leaders. All too often, those seeking volunteers merely try to find somebody—anybody. Their objective: "Let's get a warm body to fill the position." The objective should be "Let's find the person most qualified for this job!"

Not only do some congregations disregard the matter of qualifications, but some actually view leadership as a way to draw in the inactives. This is not a wise course of action! Rarely is a lukewarm member able to lead others effectively.

Congregations should take into consideration people's personalities, interests, experiences, talents, and commitment when asking them to assume a leadership position in the church. They should make every attempt to match the servant and the task.

• *Explain what the job entails.*

Provide clear job descriptions to people who are asked to serve in positions of leadership. Outline their responsibilities and inform them about any problems associated with the particular job they are considering. Give them a realistic view of the demands. Knowing what a job entails helps a person envision the time commitment and skills required. Sometimes people accept jobs on the premise that there are minimal requirements. Those who approached them may have said, "You won't have to do very much." They are dismayed, then, if they discover that the responsibility is far more demanding than they were led to believe.

• *Choose leaders who have a willingness to serve.*

Those who assume leadership roles should never do so reluctantly or out of a sense of obligation. Unless a person wants to do a job and feels some sense of interest and excitement, his or her efforts may not be adequate. Leadership is a high calling that requires time, training, commitment, and hard work. Sometimes leaders may even need to curtail several less important personal activities for the duration of their term of office so that their attention can be given to their church leadership responsibilities.

• *Train leaders for their new responsibilities.*

Experience shows that untrained leaders often begin with apprehension. They may waste valuable time getting started and seldom anticipate all that is required to accomplish the task. Training sessions at the outset instill confidence and provide direction. People who know what they are doing are usually more excited and also more successful.

• *Give leaders the support and respect they deserve.*

Encourage members of a congregation to affirm their leaders in several ways. Members can volunteer to help whenever possible; a ready and willing work force is an invaluable tool to a leader with ideas and goals. Members can also express appreciation for their leaders' work and undergird endeavors with prayer.

We can improve our organizational system by establishing a clear purpose for ministry, streamlining our committee structure, and strengthening leadership.

• **Goals**—Does our church have a vision statement? Does each committee have a clear purpose related to that vision statement?

• **Simplification**—Is our committee structure simple and clear? Are boundaries of responsibility clearly defined?

• **Leadership**—When leaders are selected, are their interests and giftedness taken into consideration? Are they trained and encouraged?

3

CHURCH VOLUNTEERS

Church workers are our brothers and sisters in Christ. Our challenge is to offer them meaningful ways to share their time and talents in ministry without compromising their personal needs.

Accomplishing effective ministry within the church poses unique challenges to leaders. One of those challenges is learning how to conserve human resources and use them wisely.

Consider Martha: At age 56 Martha was involved in many organizations at her church. Because she was a capable leader, her expertise was eagerly sought. Whenever a need arose, people said, "Ask Martha. She really knows how to get things done." After several years of intensive commitment to many projects, Martha felt used, unappreciated, and too worn out with church work to hear the Lord's bidding in her own heart. Fatigue clouded her prayer life. Resentment and growing depression robbed her

of joy in the Word. Her disappoint-
ment with the community of believers
had deeply affected her faith. She was
completely frazzled and found it necessary to withdraw altogether from active life at church. Did members care?
    Oh, yes. They grumbled and simply couldn't
understand why she left. Some said she might be
having marital problems. Others speculated about
possible financial problems in the family or other
causes for her retreat. No one suspected volunteer
burnout. Soon her roles were filled by other volunteers, and Martha was forgotten.

Like many believers, Martha joined the church primarily to grow in Christ and follow Jesus. She wanted to
know and do God's will and serve by using her abilities
and resources in Kingdom work. Unfortunately, Martha's
church took advantage of her willingness and disre-
garded her growing signs of fatigue and distress.

    Is your church guilty of encouraging members to
spread themselves thin for good causes? Committee
responsibilities should not require so much time that
volunteers sacrifice family or health by spending all
spare moments doing church work. We all need to
remind each other that organizations are a means to an
end, not ends in themselves. Congregations should encourage members to select service opportunities with
care and to balance service with personal spiritual
growth.

    As we seek to improve our organizational activity,
we might begin to look for ways to make service more
pleasant. We often overlook the fact that most church
work is done by volunteers. Volunteers are generous
people who donate time, talent, ideas, money, and
effort; they want to make a meaningful contribution. If
we survey most congregations, however, we are likely
to find that growing numbers of volunteers are disheart-
ened. They are confused about their responsibilities, are

assigned tasks outside their interest areas and gifted-ness, are given little or no training, and are guided by unimaginative leaders. No wonder a high level of frus-tration and discouragement pervades some churches!

If we can overcome these obstacles, volunteers can become more effective and derive greater satisfaction from their service. The first step is to identify conditions that may hinder and discourage workers.

HINDRANCES TO EFFECTIVE SERVICE

1. Many church volunteers serve outside the areas of their own giftedness.

Result: Volunteers pressed into positions for which they are not suited can feel resentful. If they are reluctant when asked to serve, it might be because they know they have little to contribute and can foresee their dis-comfort with the responsibility. If one is gifted with teaching ability but is asked to plan a fellowship dinner, he or she may be quite uncomfortable. It may take that person longer to do the work, and he or she will prob-ably feel a great amount of anxiety in the process.

Although willingness to help is the first requirement for service, it is not the only consideration. Volunteers are most effective if they can serve in areas where they feel they can make a significant contribution. In Ephesians 4, Romans 12, and I Corinthians 12, Paul underscores the fact that we are all gifted differently so that Christ's Body, the Church, is more fully equipped for ministry.

A congregation should celebrate the diversity of its members—diversity in experience, interest, and ability. Every church should consciously seek to connect members with responsibilities that stir their enthusiasm. In this way, long-time members, as well as new members, can be assisted in identifying their special giftedness.

2. Many committee members have no clear idea of their responsibilities.

Result: Much time is wasted in confusion, overlapping activities, or needless debate. Activities may take place, but too often they do not nourish the church's spiritual vitality.

Every committee should be given a clear job description—an outline of responsibilities. This helps members be productive with their time. We live in a society that is always on the go. Not all of our busyness is purposeful, however. A committee, like society, may be swirling with ideas for activities and still miss the mark on its goals and responsibilities. The question is not, Is the Stewardship Committee doing something? Is it active? but rather, Is the Stewardship Committee fulfilling its responsibilities and achieving its goals?

3. Many volunteers have vivid memories of new ideas in the church that failed or caused hurt feelings; they do not want to risk rejection.

Result: Because volunteers fear failure or criticism, they are tempted to take the safe approach. They fear that if they make changes, their action might destabilize the church or imply criticism of past leaders or programs. Therefore, their ideas for the future become mired in timidity.

Effective leaders support the enthusiasm of volunteers. They promote innovative thinking and do not encourage maintenance of the status quo. Before long, the underlying spirit of service becomes, "We can do better—and we are not afraid to try."

4. Most volunteers begin their duties without a committee history.

Result: Too many committees reinvent the wheel year after year.

The purpose of keeping detailed records of a committee's experience is not to provide outlines so that activities can be duplicated year after year. Instead, such records are important timesavers that can enable each successive group to learn from their predecessors. These may be called reports, minutes, or simply, paper trails.

Congregations should encourage good record keeping, including committee journals. Every event or activity planned by a group should be carefully described in writing. For example, if a September picnic is planned to usher in the beginning of a new Sunday School year, notes about how soon to begin planning and records of attendance, games, food, and other activities will provide invaluable help to those planning the event the following year. They can review the precedents, evaluate what was done, and then make changes and improvements instead of starting from scratch.

TIPS FOR IMPROVEMENT

1. Value diversity! Effective committee leaders value the willingness of volunteers to give of their time and energy. They view the diversity of opinions and background experiences of members as a creative pool from which to draw fresh water. Different personalities bring new perspectives to problem solving. Some members are visionaries, while others work best with implementation. Some bring quiet wisdom, while others bubble with enthusiasm and creative thinking. The effective leader is like an artist with a palette full of exciting colors. The challenge is to create a beautiful painting by using diverse resources skillfully.

2. Acknowledge needs! Realize that volunteers have legitimate expectations. Volunteers hope they are giving something to their church when they serve on a committee. Indeed they are! They are giving time, energy, talent, and ability. However, every volunteer also has a right to receive certain things back from the church. We might regard these as "satisfaction wages," which include

• *Work satisfaction*—Leaders have to reinforce volunteers' sense of satisfaction in their work. Volunteers need to feel that their contribution is meaningful (making a difference) and that the work they are doing is worth the effort.

• *Time satisfaction*—Volunteers need to feel that their time is being invested wisely and that meetings are productive. Effective meetings energize participants and enable them to accomplish their tasks. Unfortunately, too many meetings are simply a waste of time.

• *Value as persons*—Volunteers need to feel valued as individuals, not just as workers. People feel used when no one cares about them personally. Committee meeting agendas should allow time for interaction and care concerns. Before the business agenda begins, members should spend time getting in touch with each other. This can be a time of sharing significant personal or family events since the group's previous meeting. Some may voice special prayer requests. Sharing time may conclude with a prayer incorporating those requests mentioned by the members. Group members should feel valued—first, as beloved children of God and fellow believers, and only second, for their contribution as workers. A sense of godly love and caring should permeate every undertaking of the church. Otherwise, one is likely to hear more than a few say, "Why should I care about this church when it doesn't care about me?"

• *Appreciation*—Celebration should be a part of every committee's experience. When major tasks are completed, credit should be given to workers and joy in that group's achievement shared. The church's work never ends. If there are no pause points for celebrating successes along the way, volunteers are likely to get discouraged. We owe them a sense of accomplishment rather than the guilt and burden of feeling there is always more to be done.

 To build a happy and effective work force within a congregation—

- Encourage people to work in areas of their interest and giftedness.
- Value your volunteers, and make the time they spend in meetings worthwhile.
- Pause along the way to celebrate achievements.

4

ORGANIZATIONAL STRUCTURES

An organization's structure is effective if volunteers feel joy in ministry and accomplish their goals.

Surely a church with many committees and workers must be a healthy church. *Not necessarily!*

The question is not, How many people in the church are involved in committees? but, How effective are those committees? In fact, excessive organization may be counterproductive. It can sap members of energy for mission and personal growth.

As a preliminary step to devising an effective organizational structure, it is helpful to consider several alternative ways of thinking with regard to general practice. Some of our traditional patterns may be outmoded. If we consider other perspectives on the "basics," we may discover that even small changes can improve organizational vitality.

RETHINKING TRADITION

TERMINOLOGY

Historically, the word *committee* has been used to designate church work groups. Although *committee* is an acceptable term for some people, it can have negative connotations in the minds of others. People who are asked to serve on a committee sometimes hesitate because of past experience with long, non-productive meetings. Church members often view committee work as self-perpetuating, institutionalized activity. Committee members seldom envision themselves as strategizers or agents of change.

Therefore, one suggestion for establishing an effective organizational structure is to minimize use of the word *committee* for primary groups. Substitute other terms. For example, standing committees could be called *boards*. Instead of serving on the Worship Committee, members would serve on the Board of Worship. Use of the term *committee* will be minimized throughout the rest of the book.

Find creative names for secondary groups as well. *Team* is a word that implies action as well as cooperative effort. The Altar Team would have clear, action-oriented goals related to worship. The Vacation Bible School Team would have clear, action-oriented goals related to education and community mission. In other words, much of the hands-on work of your church would be done by service teams assembled for clear and specific purposes.

The point is that people's concept of committees has been damaged by overuse and a history of tedium and ineffectiveness. Review and revision of nomenclature may be a first step toward infusing structure with new life.

TERMS OF SERVICE

Tradition dictates that church volunteers serve on an annual basis; however, many tasks do not require a twelve-month or multiyear commitment. Church members who are harried and busy in the workplace might be willing to concentrate on a specific task for a short period of time. Considering the surge in travel, scheduling uncertainties, and increasing numbers of dual-vocation households and single-parent families, a congregation should offer creative alternatives to long-term service. Encourage people to focus their energies on given tasks for a month, three months, or whatever time is needed to complete the work. Asking for short-term commitments is especially wise in small churches where the volunteer pool is limited or in larger churches where there has been volunteer burnout. Flexibility in work assignments makes it possible for members to contribute who otherwise might not do so.

Translated into practical example, it is better to involve Mary for six weeks in directing the Sunday School Christmas program than to burden her with a year's commitment to parish education meetings that she cannot possibly fit into her busy schedule. Enthusiastic service for a short time is better than nonparticipation for the long term.

MEETING TIMES

Tradition also dictates that most work groups meet monthly; however, not all church groups need regular meetings. Furthermore, groups do not always have to meet on weeknights. Breakfast meetings, Saturday brown-bag meetings, or other creative solutions to time constraints help ease the need for baby sitters and offer flexibility to those with conflicting work schedules.

VALUE AND PURPOSE

Once a board or team is created, it often exists in perpetuity. Structure should not be set in stone with automatic annual renewal. Regular evaluation of congregational needs will help maintain a structure that is simple, effective, and responsive to current needs.

When business leaders consider projects, they usually ask the question, "Is it cost effective?" When evaluating organizational structure, church leaders should ask, "Is it people effective?"

A church risks stagnation if its organizational structure remains unchanged for a five-year period. All operating levels should be subject to regular evaluation. Some groups may need to be combined because their responsibilities are closely related. Other groups may need to be disbanded because they no longer serve a useful purpose, are ineffective, or have become a vehicle for discord.

REDESIGNING STRUCTURE

Our goal is to devise a simple, overall structure. Various models of organization exist and can be successfully used, but most congregations use a structure that includes a supervisory board, midlevel planning groups, and short-term service teams. The following example shows how to streamline this familiar and traditional pattern to make it more effective.

GOVERNING BODY

Every church needs a governing body to oversee total ministry of the congregation. Authority is necessary to produce unified, forward movement. This group may be called the Vestry, Council, Session, Administrative Body, or simply, the Governing Body. However named, its duties include planning, supervising, coordinating, and evaluating the church's overall ministry.

Focus—The governing body must focus on the church's vision statement. Simply stated, the governing body of a church guides members and teams toward the accomplishment of their church's overall goal. Whereas secondary groups focus on specific aspects of ministry, the governing body focuses on the big picture to assure unity of action and monitors progress.

Duties—Church constitutions describe specific duties of governing bodies, but generally speaking, duties should include

- establishing the congregation's annual goals in accord with the vision statement
- coordinating church programs so that work is purposeful
- approving unbudgeted expenditures or program changes that affect everyone
- supporting and encouraging pastors and salaried staff
- overseeing policies, contracts, and budgets
- monitoring attendance and contribution records
- evaluating overall programming and staffing
- doing long-range planning

The governing body should not do the work of implementation. For example, it should not plan stewardship programs, recruit teachers for parish education, or plan fellowship dinners. Its main challenge is to guide and support all church efforts toward accomplishment of the vision statement.

The governing body is like a parent planning meals for the family. The parent doesn't necessarily have to do the shopping, cooking, and clean-up chores alone, but he or she must at least plan menus, enlist the help of family members, encourage efforts, and supervise the process.

Membership—The governing body consists of the church's elected officers and chairpersons representing the congregation's major ministry areas.

Officers: President, Vice-President, Secretary, Treasurer *Chairpersons:* This list will vary depending on the size of the church but may include those in charge of worship, education, outreach, administration, service, and congregational life.

All of these persons should be selected for their interest, giftedness, or experience in the areas where they will serve. They should not be elected randomly and then assigned positions. With random placement, there is a risk that programming in a particular area may suffer the entire year because the person in charge lacks experience or interest.

Meeting Times—A governing body needs to meet monthly because of the scope and importance of its work. In larger churches, quarterly planning retreats might be advisable to supplement monthly meetings; times apart in a relaxed environment often enable members to relate to each other better and be more creative in their thinking.

Boards

Boards function much like a governing body in that they are supervisory in nature. Their focus, however, is a single ministry area. Whereas a governing body looks at the whole pie, each board takes one piece of the pie and seeks to carry out effective ministry. Boards plan, coordinate, and evaluate all that happens in their particular areas of ministry, but they usually rely on others (e.g., teams) to implement their goals.

All organizations, activities, or programs in a church must be accountable to at least one of the major boards. Any new groups forming in a congregation should know exactly where they fit into the overall picture in terms of mission and accountability. Liaison provisions are essential. No group should operate without coordination with the main organizational structure of the church.

Focus—These groups develop programs. Responsibilities of each one should be clearly delineated so as to avoid overlapping or confusion. Most congregations can divide their work into six basic areas: worship, education, congregational life, outreach, administration, and service. (Terms such as *evangelism* or *witness* could be used instead of *outreach*; *nurture* or *fellowship* could replace *congregational life*.)

Duties—The number of major boards and the names given to them are not as important as the fact that they must incorporate all ministry areas of the congregation and have their responsibilities clearly defined.

Some congregations prefer to designate a special board for youth; however, churches do not usually create special boards for other groups such as senior citizens or married couples. Youth, like all ages, need worship, education, fellowship, and so on; it may be best to integrate their needs and abilities within all aspects of congregational life rather than to separate them from the rest of the body. The following list of boards does not neglect youth but sees them as an integral part of the whole.

Worship, Music, and the Arts

Responsibility for activities related to worship, such as music, Altar Guild, liturgical art and seasonal decorations, ushers and acolytes, festival celebrations, drama, and similar projects.

Education

Responsibility for study opportunities offered on a regular basis, such as Sunday School, Vacation Bible School, confirmation, and midweek programs.

Outreach

Responsibility for all activities related to nonmembers, such as visiting the unchurched, visiting prospective members, planning new-member receptions, advertising, community service, and ecumenical activities.

Congregational Life

Responsibility for all activities that nurture the members, such as fellowship events, retreats, seminars, Bible study and prayer groups, support groups, and organizations for men, women, or youth.

Service

Responsibility for matching people's abilities, interests, and experiences with opportunities for service by teaching on spiritual gifts, helping newcomers find a place to serve, and encouraging all members to participate in the church's ministry. Activity could include community volunteer work, bereavement care, tape ministry, crisis ministry, and visits to the home-bound and hospitalized.

Administration

Responsibility for managing the church's operation in terms of property, finances, personnel, and policy.

DIVISION OF RESPONSIBILITIES
Pattern A: Six Supervisory Boards

ADMINISTRATION	OUTREACH
• property • finances • personnel • policy	• visits to prospective members • new-member receptions • visits to the unchurched • ecumenical activities • advertising

WORSHIP, MUSIC, ARTS	CONGREGATIONAL LIFE
• music • altar guild • special services/festivals • ushers and acolytes • liturgical art • drama, musical productions	• fellowship • retreats • organizations • small groups: singles, youth, Bible study, support groups

EDUCATION	SERVICE
• Sunday School • Vacation Bible School • confirmation • special events	• community service • bereavement care • tape ministry • spiritual gifts • crisis ministry • visits to shut-ins

Recommended for Midsize Congregations (over 200)

Pattern B: Four Supervisory Boards

NURTURE	WORSHIP/EDUCATION
• small groups • fellowship • organizations • visits to shut-ins • bereavement care	• music • worship assistants • parish education • special events
ADMINISTRATION	OUTREACH
• maintenance • personnel • finances • policy	• unchurched • inactives • community service • new-member receptions

Recommended for Small Congregations
(Less than 200 members)

Membership—The chairperson of a board is elected by the congregation for a specific term of office. Other members may be selected by the chairperson based upon their ability or interest in the particular ministry task. Chairpersons should strive for a fifty-fifty mix of persons who have already served and members who are new to the board. This encourages fresh thought while not abandoning experience.

Meeting Times—Regular monthly board meetings will probably be needed. They do not always have to be on weeknights when parents of young children prefer to be at home.

Boards should minimize requests that team chairpersons under their supervision also attend board meetings. Sometimes people who enjoy some aspect of team ministry drop out when asked to give time to additional meetings.

> *Consider Julie:* She chairs the Altar Guild Team and meets regularly with her workers for training, encouragement, evaluation, and advance planning. Under her direction the Altar Guild members work competently and dependably. Julie not only enjoys her own turn in the rotation, but she gains satisfaction from enabling others to undergird the pastor's work in leading the Sunday morning worship experience. She is conscientious and takes great pleasure in doing her best.
>
> Julie would be happy simply chairing her team. Instead, she finds herself burdened by a request to attend monthly Board of Worship meetings as well. Finally, unable to expend the additional time, Julie resigns as chairperson of the Altar Guild Team.

Is Julie's presence really essential at Worship meetings every month, or could she meet with them quarterly or even semiannually? Could one member of the Board of Worship attend Altar Guild Team meetings occasionally? Could Julie communicate regularly by telephone with the Worship chairperson to relay concerns or receive input? Perhaps her energy is best used "on task" with the Altar Guild Team rather than as a reluctant participant on the Board of Worship. We need to conserve our human resources. Team leaders should not be required to meet monthly with their umbrella boards. They should, however, make some liaison provisions so that they are accountable to a supervisory board.

TEAMS

Focus—Teams are secondary groups with very specific and focused duties. Two basic types of teams exist: those related to ongoing needs and those that address short-term needs within the congregation. Examples of ongoing groups include music teams, altar guilds, and home visitation teams. Ad hoc team groups are formed to complete specific assignments in a limited period of time and might address such needs as constitutional review, building programs, and personnel changes.

Duties—Ministry teams are often given an idea or a responsibility by supervisory boards and then asked to figure out implementation strategies.

> *Example:* Suppose the Board of Congregational Life feels that the congregation needs more fellowship. Group members decide that a major congregational event—a picnic in the fall—would be advantageous. Its purpose would be to provide an informal setting and games so that members could get to know each other better and so that new members could become integrated into the fellowship. A picnic team would then be assembled to plan the event in accord with the purposes outlined.

> *Example:* The Board of Education feels that Vacation Bible School is important. It assembles a team to set a date, recruit and train staff, choose materials, and conduct the program.

Membership—Members are usually appointed or invited by leaders to serve. Some teams require very few workers; others may require many.

Meeting Times—Some ministry teams meet only as long as it takes to accomplish their assigned ministry tasks and to evaluate them when work is concluded. Other teams do ministry tasks that continue all year. Although all teams should stay in close contact with their supervisory boards, their members should not be required to attend additional monthly meetings. A representative from the team could report to the board chairperson or attend a quarterly meeting designed for planning the next three months.

RECLAIMING EXCELLENCE

Organizational excellence requires an enthusiastic and capable work force. The guidelines below can assist leaders in developing such a work force.

1. *Encourage the nominating team to choose candidates for positions on the governing body based upon their interests and abilities.*

2. *Give the congregation a list of major boards with a simple statement of purpose by each. Ask members to volunteer in ministry areas where they have interest, giftedness, or experience.* Make clear that these are major responsibilities requiring a considerable time commitment. Chairpersons will then select members for their boards from the list of volunteers. Assemble at least five members and no more than eight members (plus the leader) for each board. Be sure to include both men and women, various ages, people who have served before and people who have not.

3. *Provide the congregation with a list of people willing to serve on ministry teams—groups that focus on specific*

tasks and may require only a short-term commitment.
This list of volunteers will be used as a major
resource when ministry teams are formed.

4. *Begin the year with a training session for all members of
   the governing body and all board members.* Initiate the
   year with a seminar covering such topics as the
   church's vision statement, overview of board responsibilities, skills involved in small group work, goal
   setting, and planning.

5. *Maintain a sense of corporate endeavor as the year
   progresses.* If teams or boards meet on the same night
   each month, have a joint opening. If they meet at
   different times, have a fellowship time quarterly or
   biannually. At that time, leaders will review the vision statement, note progress, and express appreciation to the workers.

  To strengthen your organizational structure—

• Encourage members to work in areas of their interest and giftedness.
• Review structure regularly; search for ways to streamline and limit the number of boards.
• Allow the governing body to concentrate on the big
  picture—overall progress toward the congregation's annual goal.
• Allow each board to focus on *one* aspect of congregational activity. Members will have full responsibility for planning, supervising, staffing, and
  coordinating activities that relate to their focus
  area.
• Use ministry teams to work on specific areas of
  service. Look for ways to free volunteers to spend
  time on tasks rather than in meetings.

5

DESIGNING EFFECTIVE
MEETINGS

An effective meeting engages all members, is purposeful and productive, and gives those present a sense of forward movement.

"When can we meet to plan the new-member reception?" "Is the Worship Board meeting Tuesday night?" "Let's plan the Council agenda this evening." Meetings, meetings, meetings!

The average congregation engages its members in more than one hundred hours of meetings a month. Imagine! If that figure seems high, consider the statistics. Most churches have at least ten committees with a minimum of five members each. If these fifty people meet for two hours monthly, they will be giving one hundred hours of their time. Over a twelve-month period, twelve hundred hours will be spent. Shouldn't those hours be productive? One large congregation had fifty committees. Recognizing that much of the work was being duplicated, its council formed yet another committee to study the situation and find a solution!

Committees *are* important because they engage people in ministry. Since people must set aside time for meetings in order to do group work, the quality of that time spent becomes an issue.

Why are meetings often a waste of time and a source of frustration? Consider the following examples:

Case #1

Jenny prepared an agenda for the meeting and was excited about her first gathering with the Youth Board. She opened with a question she thought would allow everyone some input. "I'm sure all of you have ideas about what we could do to improve our youth program. You've probably been thinking about this as much as I have. What are some of your ideas?"

Unfortunately, from that point on the meeting was out of control. Some began telling stories of youth activities when they were teenagers. Others had a discouraging litany of past failures in the congregation's recent history. Since it was her first meeting with the group, Jenny was afraid she might offend someone if she closed the discussion and drew the group back to the agenda. The evening ended on a negative note. A feeling of discouragement prevailed because nothing was accomplished.

Case #2

Tom chaired the Property Board. A prime piece of land adjacent to the church had become available for purchase. He was excited about sharing this news with his board because many longed to expand present facilities. He planned his agenda as usual—reports, old business, new business, etc. Unexpectedly, a major discussion arose over an item of old business, and it took almost an hour of meeting time. As the evening wore on, people grew tired. By the time Tom brought up the availability of land, members were mentally finished and ready to go home. The matter was tabled.

Case #3

Karen joined the Stewardship Board because she really wanted to share some ideas from her previous congregation. She had participated in a dynamic program that was very successful. She arrived at her first meeting eagerly awaiting a chance to share her ideas; however, the chairperson had already prepared a detailed plan for a stewardship drive and introduced it to the Board with the words, "Don't you think this will be great?" What could Karen say? Obviously, planning the work was not going to be a board endeavor; it appeared that the group was assembled merely to ratify the chairperson's ideas. Her enthusiasm evaporated.

Why were these meetings frustrating? In Case #1, the problem was weak leadership; Jenny failed to take control of the situation and bring participants back to the agenda. Poor planning was the problem in Case #2; Tom used an agenda that placed the major item at the end of the meeting when energy of members had diminished. In Case #3, leader domination prevented the effective use of Karen's experience and ability.

What, then, is an effective meeting? It is a gathering in which all members have a chance to contribute, one that has a clear plan and direction, and one that leads to action.

INGREDIENTS FOR SUCCESS

1. *Meetings take place in a comfortable location.*

Uncomfortable furniture or temperatures affect a person's ability to concentrate. An effective leader arrives early enough to turn on thermostats and arrange the room.

2. *Time covenants are observed as much as possible.*

A meeting begins and ends on time. If the leader antici-pates a lengthy meeting, that likelihood is mentioned at the beginning. If members know there is a heavy work-load, they are more likely to avoid side roads in discus-sion.

3. *Carefully planned beginnings set the tone for business.*

Meetings begin with a positive and meaningful open-ing. Devotions centered on personal Christian growth are certainly an appropriate way to launch the meeting. Creative planning can make these moments relevant to the concerns of the meeting. Another way to begin is to provide a short opportunity for personal sharing by the group. Time spent learning about each other's concerns enhances relationships. Following any beginning activ-ity, the leader opens the meeting in a positive manner. Smiles and enthusiasm provide a warm welcome for members. The leader creates excitement about the work at hand by displaying energy and an upbeat attitude.

4. *Meetings have purpose.*

Meetings should occur because they are necessary, not because they are monthly routines. There should al-ways be a valid reason to gather. The leader engages members in meaningful discussion and decision mak-ing. Those attending thus feel a sense of accomplish-ment.

5. *An agenda is used and given to all participants.*

An agenda is given to members, preferably in advance, so that they can think about the issues to be discussed. Agendas may include scheduling and planning of events, reports, assignment of tasks, evaluation of recent activi-ties, or announcements. These meeting outlines help participants realize the scope of the business at hand so that they will not spend an inordinate amount of time on a single item early in the meeting.

6. *The most important or complicated topic is placed toward the beginning of the agenda.*

People concentrate best and have more energy at the beginning of a meeting. If there is a major item requiring action and discussion, it is introduced before members become tired and unable to focus. Less important matters can follow.

7. *Members are given time and freedom to contribute.*

A leader does not dominate discussion nor allow any members to do so. It is important that all have opportunity to think and share ideas and know that they will be heard.

Disagreement is likely to occur at times. What is important is how it is handled. Healthy debate helps a group avoid needless errors in decision making. A leader helps clarify positions so that the group can reach consensus. It is important to encourage lively exchange, but it is also necessary to stress compromise and mutual support once a decision is made.

8. *A positive spirit prevails as the work of the church is undertaken.*

Effective leaders always look for ways to encourage committee members and express gratitude for tasks well done. There is a saying, "Nothing succeeds like success." When volunteers feel their work is appreciated and important, they are encouraged to continue.

9. *Action is taken.*

Members derive satisfaction from making decisions and taking action. They leave with a sense of accomplishment and feel that time was well spent because new directions will be taken as a result of their collective work.

10. *Meetings include a look at the past as well as a look to the future.*

At least quarterly, all working groups should make notes of what has been successful thus far and what they would do differently if they could turn back the clock. Without these helpful notes, our experiences cannot guide us in the future. Time may be given to future events as well. Upcoming dates or needs are mentioned so that proper planning can be done. We all need reminders! Occasionally, time should be given to long-range planning—looking ahead with creative ideas.

Remember: A church member should come away from group work with a sense of being valued and needed, a clear understanding of responsibilities, and a conviction that time is being spent productively because the group's accomplishments are evident. Nothing less is acceptable. We are stewards of our human resources in the church. Time and talents of our members must be used wisely and never wasted in boring, nonproductive meetings.

Congregations need to strive for excellence in conducting their business. We can no longer afford to be lazy, ill-prepared, and apathetic about the programs of the church. Dynamite programs do not just happen. They are produced by efficient and dedicated volunteers, pastors, and staff.

6

THE PASTOR'S ROLE

A pastor's role in organizational work is that of a coach, cheerleader, and trainer. The pastor equips and supports leaders so that they can accomplish tasks of ministry more effectively.

The pastor has a big job—serving people who have varied expectations of the pastoral office based on their own past experiences or current needs. Facing endless demands on personal energy, the pastor makes difficult decisions every day regarding time management. Since committee work often takes a significant amount of time from the weekly calendar, both pastor and congregation need to agree on what role the pastor will play in organizational work.

INEFFECTIVE PASTORAL ROLES

Floating Ambassador—Sometimes pastors opt for the role of floating ambassador—one who drifts in and out of meetings just to be seen, to lend support, or to influence whenever possible.

This role is ineffective because a pastor who merely pops in and out of meetings cannot possibly understand the thinking of the group; nor can members of that board fully grasp a pastor's ideas on the spur of the moment. If a pastor does not have regular contact with group leaders and only attends meetings sporadically, that pastor can expect frustration, disappointment, and possibly embarrassment. Lack of involvement prevents the pastor from influencing program decisions, sharing problem-solving tasks, encouraging workers, and being well informed.

Executive Director—Some pastors opt for the role of executive director. They direct council and board work with zeal and dominate meetings. They exert such influence that boards seek their approval for all decisions and often feel unable to proceed if the pastor cannot attend a meeting. In such a context, the pastor initiates most of the action, and the group carries out the pastor's wishes.

The obvious drawback to such a role is that laypersons do not develop strength or confidence. Because they become dependent upon the pastor for ideas and solutions to problems, they do not take responsibility themselves by engaging in creative thinking; neither do they feel a sense of victory when goals are accomplished because they attribute success to the pastor. Furthermore, if that pastor moves to another parish, the boards and leaders left behind will feel helpless and confused.

Detached Observer—Occasionally pastors choose not to participate in board work at all unless a crisis arises. As long as programs work, they do not interfere or advise but choose to invest time in other ministry tasks.

Council and board members in such a congregation may feel that the pastor is not especially interested in their work and that their efforts are unappreciated. Furthermore, if the pastor is unaware of their plans and activities, duplication of effort may occur, producing frustration. With all boards operating independently and thus without cohesiveness, a congregation cannot take significant steps forward in unified ministry.

Clearly, the various roles described represent extremes in the spectrum of choice available to a pastor. Many pastors drift in and out of these roles. At times they are actively involved in board work; at other times, they withdraw due to lack of time or interest.

Consider two examples of pastoral leadership:

> Pastor Markham left Abiding Savior two years ago. He was outgoing and enthusiastic. His excitement and giftedness lay primarily in administration. He loved to be creative, to supply countless new ideas to boards and teams, to stir members with his enthusiasm for new programs, and to encourage workers along the way. Boards depended upon Pastor Markham. Indeed, he supplied far more ideas than they could possibly implement. He rarely missed meetings because he felt the action there was crucial to expanded life and ministry in the church. Some members complained, however, that he was seldom available for personal help or counseling and rarely made home visits.

> Pastor Johnson, who is Pastor Markham's successor, is also outgoing and enthusiastic, but his giftedness is in teaching, preaching, and counseling. His sensitivity, compassion, and wisdom are deeply appreciated by members. They are stirred by his sermons and challenged by his continuing exhortations to be faithful. Sometimes, however, they get frustrated by his lack of attention to programming. Pastor Johnson recognizes the importance of organizational work but simply feels his expertise lies in other areas. He encourages board members and appreciates their hard work, but he finds other ministry tasks more pressing and important than board meetings.

Which pastor effectively fulfills his responsibility with organizational groups? Probably neither! Both pastors have special gifts of ministry and use them well, but neither handles administrative leadership in a way that equips and strengthens laypeople. One exerts too much influence on boards; the other exerts too little.

Pastor Markham's gifts for administration are a blessing to his flock, but if he can use his enthusiasm to train others, he will improve the effectiveness of his leaders. If he involves others in planning, encourages their ideas, and allows them to implement programs, he will help them gain confidence and ability. His first challenge, then, is to model leadership by example and teach others his skills; his second is to address those areas of ministry he has previously neglected.

Pastor Johnson's gifts of preaching, teaching, and counseling are a blessing to his congregation, but it is important that he also be a participant in board activities. His challenge is to keep abreast of organizational needs, to find ways to be more involved, and to seek helpful resources to assist board members when they need help on matters outside his expertise.

Organizational work has long been a gray area of pastoral responsibility. Most people would agree that a pastor's primary role in a congregation is to nurture and equip the saints for ministry through teaching, preaching, counseling, and caring. In addition to those activities, however, the pastor also serves as chief administrator and motivating force behind organizational life. Why? Because the organizational structure of a church surrounds the pastor. It is the environment in which a pastor ministers. Viable ministry cannot occur if the pastor abdicates administrative responsibility.

Nevertheless, questions abound. How much time should a pastor invest in board work? Should the pastor attend all board meetings? How can the pastor influence but not dominate board work? (Many times a pastor who is present at a board meeting actually supplants the designated leader. Members look to the pastor for approval of their ideas rather than to each other or to the designated chairperson.) How does a pastor who is not an idea person undergird and support group work? Should the pastor be the chief problem solver in the church?

A MORE EFFECTIVE ROLE: TEAM TRAINER

A pastor can be most effective as one who equips members. Like a coach, a pastor trains the team. He or she empowers others to accomplish tasks of ministry by advising, encouraging, and helping them. In short, a pastor's primary role in organizational work is to equip others. The process is a long-term investment in people.

Pastors do not equip others by telling them what to do or how to do it or by attending every meeting. Even if a pastor's primary gift lies in the area of administration, he or she must resist the temptation to run the show and instead encourage others to take responsibility.

One man who served as pastor of a church for thirty years did everything from ordering bathroom tissue to writing policy for use of the organ. When he left, members did not know how to do anything. They were at a total loss about how to operate the church during the months following his departure. For years afterward, new pastors faced the problem of members expecting the pastor to do everything. The congregation had been made weak by a pastor who dominated.

The pastor does equip others by patiently helping them. He or she can impart leadership skills that will help chairpersons become more effective. If the pastor trains and encourages leaders, their confidence will spark a growing excitement for organizational work.

The pastor is a supervisor who maintains an overall view of needs and problems. As that pastor communicates with leaders, they become the specialists who find solutions and develop new strategies. A pastor certainly can assist in finding solutions and strategizing, but helping leaders to develop those skills through training will free pastors to do other tasks of ministry more effectively.

A PASTOR'S RESPONSIBILITIES
WITH BOARDS

As one who equips others, a pastor has four duties:

* to help workers remain focused on goals
* to assist in planning
* to participate in the process of evaluation
* to provide training for workers

For the most part, all of these responsibilities can be accomplished outside board meetings as the pastor invests time with the congregation's leaders. Within the context of actual meetings, the pastor should be a resource but never a dominating force.

MAINTAINING FOCUS

An effective pastoral leader keeps the congregation focused upon its goal. Pastoral vision takes in the whole scope of activity in the congregation. Like a person seated on a football stadium's top row, the pastor has a panoramic view of the action. His or her job is to assess the teams' overall progress, strengths, and weaknesses. The pastor's concern is how well the teams play and, of course, the score. Always mindful of where the congregation is headed, the pastor invites workers to strategize and plan how to get there. The pastor may also have ideas for action, but his or her priority is to keep everyone focused on the goal.

Keeping workers focused on goals can be a very difficult task in some settings. Often boards move into action that is not meaningful. The pastor must call them to evaluate. How is the action contemplated going to help achieve the goal? What is its purpose?

In a football game, it is not enough that players know how to run or how to pass or how to catch the ball. They must also learn how to play as a team in order to score and to win. Group achievement is only possible when individuals see their contributions as directed toward a clear and specific goal. The effective pastor safeguards and promotes this unity of purpose.

PLANNING

Communication and shared responsibility are essential elements in church organization. Pastor and people must be in touch and in agreement about ministry, yet they do not need to take every step in unison. The challenge for pastors is to guide and support leaders but not to supplant them. How can a pastor have a voice in what transpires but not attend every meeting? How can a pastor strengthen leadership and influence without dominating?

A pastor does this by investing time with individual leaders before their meetings. This is time well spent, especially in the first quarter of a new year. These meetings allow pastor and leaders to come into agreement, to strategize, to anticipate problems before they occur, and to become mutually supportive. The pastor should try to meet with each chairperson monthly during the first quarter.

If leaders are well prepared for their committee meetings, frequent attendance by the pastor is not essential. When the pastor does attend a meeting, his or her comments are neither a surprise nor a threat to the designated leader; rather, the pastor becomes an ally and a valued resource person. As pastor and leaders develop mutual understanding and as leadership skills improve, the pastor's involvement in advance planning will be decreased but not eliminated.

The initial quarter is crucial. New leaders are developing habits, attitudes, and relationships that will influence the year's work. They are receptive to guidance and usually optimistic about the future. Furthermore, a strong beginning influences what can be accomplished. The sooner work is begun, the greater the chance of success.

By the time a second quarter begins, perhaps the pastor can work with several chairpersons together, especially if their tasks are related. Sessions will probably focus less on detailed planning and more on problem solving and creative thinking.

In the final half of the year, it may not be necessary for a pastor to meet with chairpersons every month, but regular contact of some type is still advisable. The pastor should be flexible and anticipate needs. Some persons require more help than others; some boards have more extensive responsibilities than others; some groups have activities that peak at certain times of the year and ease up at other times. A pastor should take those variables into account and be available for counsel.

Although individual meetings with chairpersons may seem time-consuming, careful planning can make the most of a short time. The hours invested in chairpersons usually save hours spent attending group meetings.

EVALUATING

As pastors evaluate, their primary emphasis is not placed upon problems. An effective pastor is positive and appreciative whenever possible and critical only in a constructive manner. Objective evaluation is an ongoing and essential tool of effective organizational life. Pastor, staff, and members alike need to be open to improvement, to new and better ways of doing things. A pastor can be a role model with this kind of evaluation.

Evaluation should occur when new programs are under consideration. Are they feasible? Are they suitable in light of the goals? The evaluation process continues once new programs are implemented. Are they accomplishing what was planned? Evaluation should certainly be done at the conclusion of an event, an activity, or a year. The pastor can encourage thinking with questions such as these: What would you have done differently? How would you change this for the next year? What were the strengths and weaknesses of the event? Did it accomplish what you had hoped?

Volunteers should be made to feel their efforts are worthwhile even though certain improvements can be made. The pastor's wider perspective often helps them solve problems and move forward.

Training

An effective pastor works closely with leaders to help them develop leadership skills and evaluate progress. Many denominations offer seminars and workshops at the regional level or provide resource people to conduct training on-site. It is helpful for leaders to attend these events together. There are books available to improve leadership skills and provide background for ministry. These can be read and discussed in a group setting such as a retreat. Pastors can encourage a retreat or seminar for new leaders early each year after elections. If the pastor does not feel able to lead the event, then he or she should assist in locating retreat leaders.

When a pastor spots a weak leader as the year progresses, the pastor can work with that person who is discouraged or floundering. In some situations, the pastor may be in the best position to offer help. In other situations, the pastor might enlist the help of another parishioner who has special expertise.

LEADER-PASTOR MEETINGS

Time spent with individual leaders is advantageous for several reasons. An exchange of ideas prior to the meeting

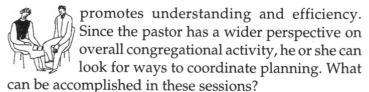 promotes understanding and efficiency. Since the pastor has a wider perspective on overall congregational activity, he or she can look for ways to coordinate planning. What can be accomplished in these sessions?

• *First, the pastor can share his or her own concerns and ideas for ministry with the leader.* In this regard, the pastor should be a generalist. The pastor might say, for example, "I see a real need to involve our children in worship. I'd like to find ways to make the worship service more meaningful to them. Do you think your board could suggest some ideas for this?" The pastor may wish to share some personal ideas for consideration by the board, or the pastor may want to hear the board's ideas first.

• *Second, the pastor can gain understanding of the leader's perspective on congregational needs.* Leaders usually welcome a time of personal consultation with the pastor. They want to share their own ideas and problems related to their particular ministry area.

• *Third, an agenda can be planned with care given to prioritizing.* As the chairperson mentions possible ideas for an agenda, the pastor may wish to add some items or have others delayed; this is a much better time to give input than in the midst of a meeting. A pastor can help with this stage of planning by seeking priorities. *Which items need action? Which ones are simply matters for preliminary discussion? Which items require work between meetings to gather information?*

Lay leaders derive several important benefits from these sessions with the pastor. One is self-confidence. After a few months of such meetings, leaders will gain confidence in planning. They will begin to generate their own ideas more easily.

They also gain a sense of being valued as a team member. Leaders will attach greater importance to their work if the pastor meets with them regularly. By going over agendas, making changes before meetings occur, clarifying priorities, sharing relational problems that may arise, and by showing interest in leaders as friends and co-workers, the pastor becomes an encourager—someone who wants the leaders' efforts to succeed and one who values their work.

In addition, leaders usually gain a much better understanding of overall ministry. From their individual meetings with the pastor, leaders can gain an understanding of the pastor's concerns, a satisfaction in sharing their own plans and ideas, a clear direction for the upcoming meeting, and a sense of excitement for the overall work of the congregation.

Advantages for pastors are equally important. One notable benefit is that time invested in meetings with leaders prior to group meetings will save the pastor hours of time in the long run. How? The pastor's attendance at every meeting will not be necessary. Hours will not need to be spent in correcting ill-advised board action. Wasted time from meetings poorly planned and managed will be minimized. Organizational work in the church will become much more efficient because leaders will be equipped to lead effectively.

Consider this: The average pastor attends at least six two-hour meetings every month. In addition, at least eight hours are spent with ad hoc group meetings. Six more hours are spent reading reports of what happened in meetings the pastor did not attend, trying to change ill-advised actions, and correcting communication problems. Surely these twenty-plus hours could be better spent if they were invested in planning with individual leaders.

Pastors also benefit by strengthening relationships with members. Time invested in helping others become successful has many rewards. Mutual understanding between pastors and laypersons advances overall ministry. The pastor will be more effective as members learn to understand and trust his or her leadership.

Finally, these sessions offer pastors an opportunity to garner support for ministry goals. Sharing concern can encourage others to help solve problems or lend aid.

JESUS' STRATEGY

Jesus had only three years of public ministry. With so many people clamoring for his attention, he had to guard his time and energy and to strategize in order to minister effectively and to accomplish his mission. Thus, although he taught the multitudes, he narrowed his focus of intensive teaching to a few men whom he chose to be leaders. He spent time teaching and equipping these twelve disciples so that they could carry on his ministry. He no doubt felt that a greater impact could be made in the long run if those who carried out the ministry were well-trained leaders. Before He died, Jesus prayed for these twelve; the prayer in John 17 concludes with these words: "I made known to them thy name . . . that the love with which thou hast loved me may be in them and I in them."

We often believe we have the greatest impact by touching the most people. We spread ourselves thin and accomplish little of significance.

Jesus had a deliberate strategy for making the most of time. Despite the strenuous demands of his public ministry, He sought time alone with the twelve disciples to instruct them, answer their questions, and pray with them. Perhaps his example could help today's harried pastor find a way through the organizational maze. The key is for pastors to spend time strengthening and upbuilding congregational leaders.

Although pastors have different gifts and priorities in ministry, they must assume a leadership role in organizational work. Their influence can be most effective if they stay in close touch and consultation with congregational leaders while attending meetings on an occasional basis.

Goals and Strategies

Section Two

CREATING A PLAN

Congregations often have many committees that operate almost independently. These committees make decisions, plan programs, and initiate major changes without considering how their plans will affect or contribute to the overall mission of the church. The average church member, in fact, may not even know the mission of the church! A church may appear to be a beehive of activity, but closer scrutiny may indicate that its activity is not fruitful. Running in many directions at once is not conducive to success. Without a clear sense of direction to guide activity, a congregation may never become cohesive enough to pursue its dreams.

Perhaps it is helpful to return to our analogy of the apple game. The apples of this childhood game are somewhat like the aspirations we have for our churches. We cannot grasp them all at once. Imagine yourself bobbing for apples. When you kneel before a huge tub filled with enticing apples, you must concentrate on one particular fruit. It could be the biggest or the prettiest or simply the closest. Whatever the attraction, you must focus on one apple at a time. If you are successful, you may go back for a second or third apple, but your mouth cannot grasp more than one at a time. The first step of strategy is choosing an objective; the second is determining an approach. In the case of apples, random dunking of the face in water seldom brings success. Moving carefully toward the apple of choice is much more effective than lunging here and there. So it is in the church. Like floating apples, many goals vie for our attention. Because there is such a range of possibilities, there is a need to choose one goal at a time and carefully develop strategies for attaining it.

Goals should be the driving force of organizations. They define purpose. They guide planning and help groups move in appropriate directions. After all, the intent of church committees is not simply to be engaged in busywork, but rather to contribute to the church's witness and forward movement. Clearly, ministry is multifaceted, but both individuals and groups within a congregation should work under the umbrella of mission. Working with goals connected to mission can revitalize group activity. Try it! Setting goals is not a boring task. On the contrary, setting goals is a dynamic activity requiring value judgments, strategy, wisdom, spirituality, and commitment.

7

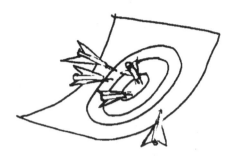

THE NEED TO FOCUS

The church must make conscious choices about ministry based on purpose and resources. A clear focus revolutionizes congregational planning.

Ministry today includes a vast array of programs. Everything from worship and educational programs to such activities as day care, food pantries, and fitness programs come under the umbrella of church management. They all require manpower and money. We have spread ourselves thin in our efforts to meet burgeoning demands. How can we possibly focus when there is so much work to be done? Of course, our youth need more attention! Yes, and we'd like to improve our choir program! No one visits the sick. Why can't we renovate the sanctuary? The list is endless; resources are limited. Therefore, we must make conscious choices in accord with Scripture and our congregation's vision statement. We must focus on our primary task.

The Church's Primary Task

The church can and should do many things but is uniquely equipped by God for one particular task—to be a source of spiritual vitality in the world. The church's primary task is to share the Gospel. Generally speaking, we could say the focus is upon proclamation—telling the story of Jesus and his love. Each congregation, however, may interpret the Great Commission in a slightly different manner in its vision statement. The next chapter will further explain vision statements. Their importance cannot be overestimated; they help us stay on course while we consider the many options for ministry.

The contemporary church is besieged with cries for help. Christians respond warmly with myriad programs. People of good heart and worthy intent run about trying to meet the needs of a floundering society. They rush to bring love where there is violence, hatred, and rejection. Is that wrong? No! Scripture clearly gives believers a mandate to work for justice and bind up the wounds of the brokenhearted. The problem is that sometimes social ministry supplants the primary task of telling the story of salvation. Deeds are an important part of our proclamation message, but they cannot become a substitute for telling the story with words.

Our challenge, therefore, is to constantly strive for creative, effective proclamation of the Gospel, while at the same time selecting programs that meet the needs of the community and relate to our congregation's vision for ministry. Jesus set an example for us in this regard. His actions were never apart from his message; they were expressions of it and clearly integrated. His ministry to the hungry, tired, sick, or downtrodden was always done in the context of his teaching. In the same way, organizational activity should always be done in the context of proclaiming the good news.

WHY WE OFTEN GET SIDE-TRACKED

We are affected by several major societal factors: complexity, change, and confusion. The church is in the world, but the world is also in the church. Trends in society weave through the fiber of Christian experience, often causing the church to continue to major in minors. If we recognize these influences, we can take corrective action.

• *Complexity*—Our world today is increasingly complex and fast paced; choices are limitless. Suggestions abound as to how life can be more exciting and fulfilling. We have, therefore, developed a habit of doing many things at once, and sometimes we do nothing very well. Even our children are affected. They often participate in so many activities that they find solitude disturbing. Choices are difficult, and consequences of choice are often unclear.

The church, like society as a whole, finds it difficult to focus. Believers, caught up in accelerated living, scurry to incorporate new programs to meet every possible  want and need, but many mediocre activities are not as effective as one powerful, unified program. Therefore, the church must begin to make choices based on its primary purpose. There is an urgent need to establish priorities.

• *Change*—Values are changing. Issues such as sexuality, social justice, abortion, and the death penalty divide our nation. What is the meaning of family in today's world? Is there a limit to first amendment rights? How do we teach respect for authority? We hear many opinions about what is right.

Paralyzed by the same confusion, the church often maintains the status quo. It opts for safety and silence rather than risk an unpopular stance. Instead, the church must help its members clarify values in the light of Scripture and risk the consequences of boldness.

• *Confusion*—Not only are we living in a fast-paced environment where values are changing, but we also are affected by technological changes in communication. We are stunned daily by news from around the world. Information is available on every conceivable subject—information that is seemingly unlimited, constantly changing, and often confusing.

Nothing is simple anymore. The government in our country reportedly needs a 300-page guideline to provide workers in an energy plant with directions for changing a light bulb. Our tax forms are so confusing that even experts come up with differing interpretations. Legal jargon seems designed to thwart the average citizen's desire to comprehend.

Lack of clarity in the written word has also invaded the church. We have become painfully aware that words can not only bless but also hurt and confuse; as we struggle to make language all-inclusive, we often produce ineffective, confusing statements. Our communication seems designed to stand up in court under intense scrutiny rather than to be a simple expression of what we are about. No wonder the average church member does not have a clear idea of the church's mission. In order to avoid confusion, the church needs to express its message with simplicity and clarity.

REGAINING FOCUS

The focus of a congregation is to be found in its vision statement. The vision statement, a definition of the congregation's purpose or mission, should be elevated to a position of prominence in organizational life. It should be a clear and concise statement—one that all ages can grasp, engrave on their hearts, and put into practice. Such a vision statement guides all other planning.

Once members adopt a vision statement, they begin to concentrate on goals. Goals reflect strategy. They set forth specific action steps to help the congregation accomplish its primary purpose. Each year the congregation's governing body sets a specific goal that is designed to advance ministry in an area deemed appropriate. This action step is called the congregation's annual goal. Such goals can be powerful tools of motivation, or they can be useless words on paper. Simply having goals does not ensure success. Goals can fail if they are not understood by members or implemented with care. Members must know why certain goals have been chosen by the leaders and how those goals will translate mission into ministry. Goals can also fail if they are inappropriate or ill-timed. Choosing an annual goal is a process requiring wisdom and prayerful consideration of alternatives.

A third way to regain focus is to establish board goals. A board establishes two types of goals: those pertaining to the congregation's annual goal and those related to its own ministry tasks. Partnership goals are action steps that will help achieve the congregation's annual goal. Ministry goals are action steps designed to bring about change in some aspect of the board's ongoing work.

Why do boards need to formulate ministry goals? Aren't they usually given a list of responsibilities? Probably, but responsibilities are different from goals. Responsibilities are designated tasks given to boards. For example, every year the Board of Parish Education is charged with recruiting staff for the Sunday School, providing training for teachers, ordering materials, planning special events, and so forth. If a board continues to fulfill its responsibilities year after year without a creative effort to evaluate and improve things, programs will not move forward. Within the framework of every board's responsibilities there are certain areas that need special attention or development; those are the ones to which a board can direct concentrated effort in the form of goals.

Goals are proposals for change. They are strategies or plans for action. They indicate that some aspect of the work does indeed need priority treatment. For example, the Board of Parish Education may wish to upgrade teaching by training the staff; a goal directed toward teacher training changes the status quo. It establishes a focus for intensified planning.

Congregations can regain focus by renewing their commitment to mission. Members will feel a sense of satisfaction when they participate in projects directed toward priority needs rather than toward those that siphon off energy in random activity. Progress is rarely accidental. It is more often the result of careful planning and adherence to goals.

Restoring a focus on mission will help the congregation establish priorities and move forward. A vision statement, congregational annual goals, and board goals all serve to engage members in active pursuit of their mission. Ministry becomes purposeful and intentional, and thus, more effective.

NOT—

8

Vision Statements

> The vision statement defines a congregation's own unique response to the Gospel. It is a unifying focus for ministry.

Believers are not all alike in the practice of their faith. Christian congregations express their common faith differently based on geographic location, denomination, age and spirituality of members, needs of the community, and many other variables. Each congregation has to define its own mission and unique calling in order to be effective in its ministry.

To put the idea in visual terms, consider the matter of putting a puzzle together. Suppose you are given a new puzzle composed of five hundred pieces. The fact that you may have done puzzles many times before would not provide significant help with the current challenge.

What would help? Looking at a picture of the whole. A picture on the lid of a puzzle box furnishes invaluable help when we try to assemble a new puzzle for the first time. If we can visualize the outcome, we can tackle the project with confidence.

In the same way, a vision statement facilitates our progress in the church by providing a description of what we want to be and do as a group of believers. Vision statements glue us together and give us a starting point of unity. Without them we would all push the programs we personally think are most important and neglect others that may have less appeal. Vision statements provide a standard for both planning and evaluation.

A congregation can most certainly function without a vision statement. People can worship and fellowship together, maintain organizations, and provide various services. But our objective is ministry that is more effective. We can no longer afford a maintenance mentality. Instead, we must be innovative and purposeful in all that we do. We have to move forward decisively and minimize frustration.

A traveler on the highway may eventually reach his or her destination without the use of a map, but the traveler who uses a map will get there faster and with far less frustration. Likewise, one who assembles a puzzle without a picture may eventually complete the project, but he or she will do so more quickly with the aid of a visual tool. In the same way, a congregation without a vision statement may indeed do worthwhile ministry, but if the people focus with clear vision upon a particular outcome, effective ministry will occur more often and with less frustration.

How do we create the map? How do we discover the picture on the lid? How do we focus?

The process of achieving focus in a complex and diverse world begins when a congregation grapples with a basic question: *What is our primary task?* Generally speaking, organizations resist the process of defining purpose. Most leaders would rather just plunge into activities and do whatever seems necessary. If, however, a congregation has a clear job description—a direction for ministry—its organizations can begin to work together.

One could ask, "Aren't all churches supposed to do the same basic thing?" Perhaps, but there are shades of difference based on location, interests and abilities of members, needs in the community, and even the age of the congregation. Most churches define mission in accord with the Great Commission, but how each one voices purpose differs. One church may say, "Our mission is to learn and do God's will." Another, "Our mission is to bear witness to God's love in word and deed." Another, "Our mission is to continue Christ's work for justice." Another, "Our mission is to make disciples of all people." All of these reflect elements of the Great Commission, but they are slightly different emphases and therefore will require different strategies for implementation. Creating a plan begins with achieving consensus on mission.

UNDERSTANDING VISION STATEMENTS

A vision statement is a clear, concise job description for a congregation. It answers the question, *What is our primary task?* It provides a unifying vision of a congregation's fundamental goal for ministry. Few churches have clear vision statements; fewer live by them.

A vision statement is entirely different from a goal. Both serve to guide planning, but they differ in nature and function.

- A vision statement describes a congregation's primary task; it is a statement of purpose. A goal describes strategy for accomplishing the vision statement; it is a plan of action.

- A vision statement is broad and somewhat abstract. A goal is specific and concrete.

- A vision statement is of long-term duration; it can guide a congregation throughout the years of its existence. Goals are of short-term duration; as we accomplish them, we replace them with new goals.

- Sample vision statement: "Our mission is to proclaim God's Word to all people." Sample goal: "Our goal is to promote Bible study by initiating a midweek study program for all ages so that our members can grow in their knowledge of God's Word."

A vision statement need not be expressed in great detail. Additional comments that explain the statement's intent in further detail can be expressed separately if leaders so desire. The vision statement itself is a directive for ministry. It must be flexible so that in successive years the leaders can interpret and apply it according to changing circumstances. The vision statement is a beginning point; everything else will emanate from this simple, clearly stated purpose.

Ideally, a congregation should write a vision statement when the congregation is formed. Unity of vision is expressed in charter documents; when such papers are available, they can be the launching point for discussion of purpose. However, if the original papers have been lost or if a vision statement has never been adopted, current members of the congregation will have to come to agreement via retreats or other gatherings. Formulation of a vision statement should be the first priority when organizational efforts get underway.

WRITING VISION STATEMENTS

PROCEDURE

Step 1: Leaders begin the process.
Plan a meeting of congregational leaders with the sole purpose of writing a vision statement. These persons should be members of the main governing body, such as

the Council, Vestry, Administrative Board, Session or whatever group has primary responsibility for guiding business of the congregation. Explain the nature of a vision statement and underscore its importance as a guide for congregational life. Discussion about the church's mission should follow. Next, give leaders a piece of paper with the following questions to stimulate thought; after they have time to reflect, ask them to complete the statement of purpose.

VISION STATEMENT WORKSHEET

What is our congregation's primary task? What is the basic and fundamental purpose for which we have organized as a body of believers? Complete the following statement.

The primary task (mission) of Good Shepherd Church is to _____

_____.

Answers will vary. One person may say, "To make disciples of all people." Someone else may say, "To proclaim the Gospel." Yet another may say, "To share God's love with others."

Ask participants to read their answers aloud. Which responses seem broad enough to describe the fundamental work of the church and clear enough to be remembered? Begin to narrow the choice. Select no more than five statements for further consideration. Polish and edit them so they can be presented to the congregation.

Step 2: The congregation responds.

Assemble the members and explain the nature and importance of a vision statement. Present the five statements suggested by the leaders and encourage discussion of them. Then invite members to submit their own

ideas in written form, using the same worksheets provided to leaders as guidelines for thought. This step can
be done in adult classes, at a retreat, or in any forum that
will allow members ample time to reflect or to ask
questions before formulating their responses. Any additional ideas are then submitted to the governing body
of the church.

Step 3: Leaders make a selection.

Leaders in the governing body assemble once more for
the purpose of choosing one single statement. Additional answers submitted by members, as well as the
five responses already chosen for consideration by the
leaders, are typed and distributed. Discussion follows
as members speak in favor of particular statements.
Voting occurs. Three statements are chosen for final
consideration. Once again discussion is held. A final
vote is taken to select a vision statement to present to the
congregation.

Step 4: The congregation votes.

The vision statement should be carefully worded so as
to be clear and concise. This statement is then submitted
to the congregation with an explanation as to why it has
been selected. Opportunity is given for questions and
discussion. Members then vote whether or not to ratify
the proposed statement.

CONTENT

Although verbosity is a sign of our age, avoid the temptation to write eloquent, lengthy statements designed to
cover every possible endeavor.

The wording of a vision statement should be concise,
simple, and very clear. Anything longer than one sentence will not be remembered. The core statement should
not be crafted to cover every eventuality; flexibility
allows future generations to interpret and apply the
statement based on current circumstances.

Jesus gave us many examples of short, clear directives:

- Love one another as I have loved you. (John 15:12)
- Make disciples of all men. (Matthew 28:19)
- Love God above all and your neighbor as yourself. (Matthew 22:37–39)
- Seek first the Kingdom of God. (Matthew 6:33)

These are simple and specific yet broad enough to cover not only the lifetime of a believer but also the lifetime of a congregation.

If a congregation feels a need to become more specific and spell out all aspects of the vision statement, such clarification can be done by writing a document of intent to accompany the vision statement. However, the vision statement itself should remain short, simple, and clear.

USING VISION STATEMENTS

Once a statement is chosen, leaders begin the process of stirring up enthusiasm and translating purpose into action. People tend to remember short sayings more easily; therefore, condense the already short statement into a catchy phrase that can be used on banners and bulletins to remind members of their mission.

One congregation selected the following vision statement, "The mission of St. John's is to share Christ's love with the community." Members shortened the concept to "Hearts for Christ" and incorporated the motto into all printed materials. First Methodist adopted as their vision statement, "Our mission is to tell others the story of salvation." They reduced the idea to three words— "Go and Tell"—and used the motto to reflect their emphasis on sharing the good news.

Promote the vision statement on bulletins and banners, study its meaning in small groups, print it on meeting agendas, use it on church stationery, make special shirts or mugs to promote the idea, or use it in television/radio publicity. Children in the Sunday School can draw pictures with their own interpretations of the message. Sermons can emphasize the idea as the new purpose is launched. If the message is communicated in a variety of ways, members will soon become excited about walking out their purpose. The vision statement becomes a rallying cry!

Begin reorganizing your church by establishing a common starting point: agree on purpose. The focus of a church determines its ministry. A vision statement guides believers in making wise choices of programs and expenditures.

9

Choosing Annual Goals

> The congregation's annual goal is a single ministry objective that will guide the congregation's life for an entire year and one that moves members toward the accomplishment of their mission.

Whereas vision statements reflect purpose for ministry, goals describe specific plans to take action. A congregation's annual goal proposes change in one specific area of corporate life and thus helps a congregation prioritize needs and become intentional about program development. It can be a powerful unifying tool capable of galvanizing members' efforts to accomplish a particular objective. The process of setting annual goals must be understood as an important responsibility and one that requires prayerful consideration of options. Goals are not simply wishes. They are not random dreams of what would be nice. They are logical, sequential action steps that help the congregation move forward to accomplish the mission described in its vision statement.

Who Determines the Annual Goal

The process of establishing the congregation's annual goal should be undertaken by the congregation's governing body because planning is unwieldy when attempted by a large number of persons. Unlike the vision statement that requires ratification by the members at large, the congregation's annual goal does not need to be submitted to members for approval. The task of setting goals and priorities is a responsibility that automatically goes with leadership. Leaders in the governing body not only set goals, but they also evaluate progress in accomplishing them. If success is evident at the end of the year, a new annual goal is adopted. If not, the current goal may be extended.

Selecting the congregation's annual goal should be the first item of business when the governing body begins a new year. As soon as new leaders assemble, they need to review the vision statement, examine progress made in achieving last year's goal, and begin to consider possible goals for the current year. Some congregations have found it helpful to set the annual goal at a meeting of both outgoing and incoming leaders. Those who are newly elected can benefit from the input of those who have more experience regarding congregational needs and activities. This is particularly true if outgoing leaders have used long-range planning to create a momentum for change; in order to communicate their ideas to their successors, they may wish to offer suggestions or proposals.

How Other Programs Are Affected

Annual goals do not preclude or replace other ministry efforts. The congregation continues to do a variety of tasks, but at the same time, it has a primary emphasis to ensure progress in an area deemed important and urgent. As members work together on a special project, boards continue to carry out their designated responsibilities with care and commitment. No work is neglected, but one aspect of work is elevated for emphasis.

Often, when one area of ministry is strengthened, others benefit as well. Enthusiasm for success tends to revitalize everyone. Why? Because the annual goal motivates people to get involved and take pride in achievement. Congregations that do not set goals are apt to conclude the year status quo—thankful if no ground has been lost but sad that no progress has been made. Goals move us forward. They help us make significant progress by forcing us to prioritize in the light of need and resources.

CHOOSING GOALS WISELY

When leaders gather to set goals, they are usually aware of many exciting options and find it difficult to make choices regarding sequence. They may view all of the ministry tasks as equally important and be tempted to make a random choice. Such action is not advisable. The particular apple we choose does make a difference. Inappropriate goals can leave people frustrated. For example, a small rural congregation struggled to acquire a fine new organ without taking into account the scarcity of trained organists. To their dismay, they were unable to find one in their sparsely populated area. Similarly, an older congregation in a declining neighborhood seemed unable to attract young families. In a desperate attempt to draw new people, members decided to paint and remodel the sanctuary. Would emphasis on developing a dynamic Sunday School or youth program have been more appropriate?

Sometimes goals under consideration are important and worthy, but the timing is not suitable due to circumstances within the group. If a congregation's membership is decreasing due to internal strife, it would probably be futile to set an outreach goal. Why would strangers want to be a part of a factious group of people? It would be better, perhaps, to work on internal relationships and then reach out to the community.

As leaders, we need to examine current conditions to see if they are conducive to success, and if they are not, we may need to postpone the main goal we have in mind and set some intermediate goals to prepare the congregation. Intermediate goals may be advisable when major changes are contemplated. These goals generally involve training, study, or relationship building; they prepare people to take future action.

Wisdom dictates that we take into consideration timeliness and feasibility when setting goals in order to avoid disappointing results.

Setting the Goal: A Multistep Process

Leaders use the vision statement as a guide for planning; they move through a multistep process that begins with visualization—creating a clear picture of what it means to accomplish mission. Vision statements are not likely to become ministry activators unless they become vivid, specific pictures of what members want to experience and do together. Once leaders can picture the objective, they can write goals.

The following hypothetical situation describes the thought process in detail, as if the congregation were setting an annual goal for the first time.

Step 1: Visualize success. What would a church that accomplishes your mission be like?

The chair of the governing body serves as facilitator and reads the vision statement to those gathered: *"The mission of First Methodist is to spread the Gospel and make disciples of all people."* The facilitator points out that the statement emphasizes outreach, and he invites those present to picture a witnessing church in specific terms. "What does this mean in your own words? Describe a witnessing church—the worship, Sunday School, and other activities. Describe the members. What signs would indicate that they possess an excitement for spreading the Gospel?"

Participants begin to create a picture of a witnessing church. One person says, "I think members would welcome strangers and really make them feel at home." Another says, "I think the worship service would be exciting, with music that involves everyone and with preaching that is warm and caring." Another, "I think there would be a strong emphasis on teaching and evangelism." Another, "I think members would be generous in working to meet the needs of people in our neighborhood." Thus, the comments flow and provide a picture of the desired outcome. One person sums up the ideas by saying, "There would be a dynamic sense of God's presence. The church would be friendly, warm, active, and involved."

Step 2: Analyze requirements. *What programs would be necessary?*

Once leaders have a clear understanding of what they want, they begin to figure out how they can achieve it. The facilitator asks, "What specific programs or activities would help us produce a witnessing church? How could people be encouraged to share their faith and reach out to others?"

One person answers, "I think we need to have a strong Bible study program so that people can learn about God's will." Another, "I think we need to help people learn how to pray." Another, "I think we need to have small groups where people can get to know each other and grow in their faith." "We need training classes to teach us how to witness." "We want support groups that help in times of difficulty." "Perhaps we could meet some of the needs in our neighborhood; I'd like to see us establish a day-care center and get more involved with the food bank." "I think our worship service should be dynamic and easy to follow so that visitors will feel welcome." "I think we need a church entrance that is accessible to the handicapped and warm and inviting to newcomers."

The facilitator lists all of these ideas on a chalkboard.

Bible study	support groups
training in prayer	service to neighborhood
small fellowship groups	dynamic, welcoming worship
training in witnessing	accessible, inviting building

Step 3: Prioritize suggestions. *Which needs are most important?*

Leaders discuss the ideas listed and rank them according to their value and ability to help develop a witnessing church. They finally identify three as most important: Bible study, dynamic worship, training in witnessing. These are considered to be essential to the development of a witnessing church and will become priorities in planning.

Leaders have narrowed choices before determining the specific area most in need of development. This shorter list of potential target areas will expedite the process of evaluating existing congregational programs.

Step 4: Examine existing programs. *How effective are current programs in these three areas?*

To evaluate existing programs in these three areas, leaders may use a question-and-answer format, or they may simply list the strengths and weaknesses of each.

Bible study—
- Are adult Bible classes relevant and dynamic? What could make them better?
- Do members take advantage of learning opportunities? If not, why not?

- Do we offer enrichment activities such as retreats, seminars, or midweek study groups?
- Are our education programs for children strong? If not, why not?

Worship—

- Is our service easy to follow?
- Is preaching relevant, making connections between Scripture and daily life?
- Are we creative in using different ways (art, drama, music, etc.) to proclaim the Word?
- Does our music program enhance worship?
- Do children find it easy to participate? If not, why not?
- Are the physical aspects (lighting, seating, condition of furnishings, etc.) of our gathering place adequate?

Training in witnessing—

- Is our mission emphasized? How?
- Do we encourage members to speak about God's work in their lives?
- Do pastors and teachers share from the heart and personalize their teaching?
- Do we have small groups where people can learn to share and trust one another?
- Do we provide any specific training in evangelism?
- How do we nurture those who do hear the Word and who join our fellowship?

From their discussion, leaders conclude that worship is fairly strong and that Bible study and evangelism training are extremely weak. They want to maintain effectiveness in worship but want to focus on either Bible study or evangelism training for special emphasis.

Step 5: Choose one focus area. *Which focus area shall we emphasize?*

Leaders now select one area of congregational ministry as a primary emphasis in the year ahead. They have narrowed their choices to Bible study and evangelism training. Which one has the strongest potential for moving the congregation in its chosen direction? Which one would logically precede the other?

They conclude that members need to know God's Word better before they can reach out effectively to others. They believe that zeal for evangelism will follow personal growth in faith. Leaders decide, therefore, to target spiritual growth first. If members become involved in Bible study, they will be strengthened in their own faith and will want to share what they have experienced.

Step 6: Strategize. What action should we take?

Leaders are ready to plan a specific action step. They ask, "How can we promote Bible study and spiritual growth?" After discussing various ideas, they come to the conclusion that small *koinonia* groups would be the best way to promote spiritual growth. These groups would meet weekly for study, prayer, and fellowship. They would help members grow in their knowledge of God's Word and in their caring for one another. As confidence and excitement grow, they would likely reach out and share with others.

Step 7: Formulate a goal. How shall we express our goal in writing?

The annual goal answers the following basic questions: *What* do we want to do? *How* shall we do it? *Why* should we do it? Leaders write the following goal: "Our goal is to promote spiritual growth by establishing small groups for study and fellowship so that we can learn God's will for us." This goal reflects a concern (spiritual growth) plus a specific action step (weekly study groups); these are coupled with a ministry objective (learning God's will).

This goal is somewhat specific but leaves detailed strategy to others. Boards will decide when the *koinonia* groups will meet, what ages will be targeted, whether transportation will be provided, and how the program will be launched. Specific guidelines for writing an annual goal are outlined in Chapter 10.

DEVELOPING LONG-RANGE GOALS

Many congregations have found it helpful to develop five-year plans or other long-range planning documents. Members can benefit from seeing a progression of thought and intention. If they understand and appreciate the proposed sequence of action steps, they will be patient in moving forward one step at a time. They will be more likely to support each step if they see the destination and ultimate objective. The following example shows how plans can be developed to cover five years.

Sample Long-Range Plan

Leaders of Chapel Hill Presbyterian Church gather to set an annual goal related to their vision statement, which states, "Our purpose is to become a loving family of God so that we can do His work." As discussion occurs, they identify several problematic characteristics of their congregation: (1) members are spread out over a large geographic area; (2) members come from different cultural and economic backgrounds; (3) families do not seem to mix much socially; their main contact with each other is at church functions; and (4) most members seem preoccupied with their own concerns.

In the light of these observations, leaders discern a need to develop a sense of community among members. They make a preliminary plan that covers five years. At the end of each year they will evaluate progress. Their plans may change, but at least they have mapped out a logical sequence of action steps. They decide to emphasize the first part of the vision statement for two years—becoming a loving family of God. After that they will work more directly with the second part of the vision statement—doing God's work.

YEAR 1—

Leaders choose the worship service as the place to begin because it has the greatest potential for impacting members. They want worship to become a time when members experience God's love and feel a warm sense of unity. Therefore, they adopt the following congregational annual goal:

> We want to make our worship service more dynamic by increasing use of music, art, drama, and lay participation so that our members can experience God's love and celebrate together.

Excitement builds as leaders plan changes in the worship service. They will emphasize the Gospel purposefully and encourage more participation by members. Special effort will be made to include sharing of faith stories, to welcome newcomers more warmly, to involve more persons in leadership and planning of the worship service, to organize rides for those who need them, and to personalize the message of salvation. They carry the idea "God loves us" as a summary of their emphasis this year and plan a special banner to be hung in the sanctuary as a visual reminder.

YEAR 2—

The second year, they will continue to work on developing community. They will maintain the changes initiated in the worship service, but they intend to shift the focus of their annual goal to fellowship groups. They will formulate an action step that will establish family activities and small groups as a way to strengthen relationships within the congregation. They will emphasize the message "We love each other" and formulate a goal directed toward building relationships.

YEAR 3—

The third year, leaders will initiate a new thrust— discovering the nature of God's work. They will write a goal related to education. Their goal will reflect the theme, "We learn about God's will for us." They will plan an action step that will expand education by providing Bible studies and retreats.

YEAR 4—

After two years of building relationships within the church family and a third year learning God's will, they hope the climate will be one of thankfulness for God's blessings and eagerness to share His love with others. Witness will be emphasized: "We share God's love by telling others."

YEAR 5—

Community needs will be addressed. Service will be the emphasis as they formulate a goal related to meeting their neighbors' needs: "We share God's love by helping others."

Note that leaders have chosen themes as an outline for long-range planning: God loves us; we love each other; we learn about God's will for us; we share God's love by telling others; we share God's love by helping others. Such themes or emphases are suitable for long-range planning, but, as was done the first year, each theme or emphasis will need to be translated into a specific annual goal, an action step connected to a ministry objective.

Long-range planning encourages a congregation to plan activities that conform to its stated vision for ministry. Concerted effort will bring about dramatic change.

The congregation's annual goal is a logical, timely action step that is part of a strategy to move members toward the accomplishment of their mission. It must be a concrete proposal for change or development. The procedure for establishing goals requires visualizing the desired outcome, analyzing key ingredients for success, evaluating the current church program, choosing a priority emphasis, and writing the goal.

10

Writing Annual Goals

> Annual goals should use clear, straightforward language to describe both an action step and a ministry objective.

In the business world, skillful presentation of a new product is almost as important as the product's development. Marketing experts must present the new product to the public in a way that stirs interest. In the case of writing a goal for the congregation, the product is not a commodity, but an idea, and careful presentation of the idea promotes acceptance in the congregation just as skillful presentation of a product promotes acceptance in the marketplace. Careful wording of a goal encourages people to support the plan.

The process of designing an effective goal requires leaders to focus on two essential components: an action step and a ministry objective. The "product" or "idea" part of the goal is *what* leaders want members to do. It is a proposal for change, an *action step*. The rationale part of the goal tells members *why* leaders want to take the action step; it is a *ministry objective*. Both components must be expressed in simple, clear language so that members understand not only what is being proposed but also the reason leaders feel the step is important.

FIRST COMPONENT: ACTION STEP

First of all, the goal contains a proposal for action. Two questions can help leaders define their intentions: *What do we want to do? How shall we do it?* By answering these questions in the goal, leaders can present members with an action step that is both clear and specific. Here are a few guidelines:

Action, Not Focus—People commonly associate goal setting with targeting an area in need of growth; in doing so, they may overlook the need to determine a specific course of action and may inappropriately substitute the idea of *focus* for *action* when writing goals. People might say, for example: "Let's focus on spiritual growth this year." "Let's work on outreach." "Let's concentrate on our youth." A focus is appropriate during the initial stages of planning when leaders are targeting a broad aspect of ministry for special attention, but in order to become a goal, the focus eventually must be translated into a specific proposal for action. Why? If a congregation hears a general emphasis instead of an action, members will not know how to respond. A focus expresses concern, but it does not suggest a strategy for change; it cannot be implemented. The first consideration in writing a goal, therefore, is to be certain the goal describes a specific action step, not a focus.

Suppose, for example, that leaders in a congregation want to find ways to address the needs of young people and to strengthen their faith; members are concerned about growing social problems related to youth. Leaders ask the first question: *What do we want to do?*

Although many options exist, their choice is to provide faith-building activities and fellowship opportunities for the young people. Since this idea is still rather broad, they ask the second question: *How shall we do it?* Again, many options exist, but they decide to initiate Sunday gatherings involving study, fellowship, and service. They write an action step describing their idea:

> Our goal is to provide a Sunday evening program that offers Bible study, fellowship, and service opportunities for our young people.

Leaders can now present to members a plan for action rather than simply a focus or concern. The goal contains a basic proposal for a new program. Related details, such as dates, time, sponsors, ages targeted, and so on, will be determined later and should not be incorporated in the goal itself.

Specific, Not General—Additionally, goals must be specific enough to engage members in action because vague ideas seldom become operational. If goals are specific, members will be able to evaluate progress and recognize success. Without specificity members will not know when they have achieved their goal and are ready to set a new one.

An example from the realm of personal experience may illustrate the value of setting specific goals. Suppose Antonio is overweight and decides to begin a diet and exercise program. He says, "My goal is to lose weight." Antonio will not know when he has reached his goal. If he instead says, "My goal is to lose twenty pounds this year," then he has a clear standard for measuring success.

The following goals are ineffective because they are not specific. The concepts are broad, and the words used are somewhat ambiguous. Many congregations pick similar goals.

1. "Our goal is to help our congregation grow."

Since growth can be envisioned as numerical or spiritual, which meaning is intended? If it is intended to mean numerical growth, it is so nebulous that one can hardly evaluate progress. When will members feel successful? An increase of one or two new members would theoretically accomplish the goal. Or is the intent of the goal directed toward spiritual growth? If so, what indicators will denote success?

2. "Our goal is to make our music program better."

Does this mean adding members to the choir, promoting congregational hymn singing, buying a new organ, purchasing additional music, or adding a bell choir? What is the criteria for determining whether or not the music program is "better"? How will the congregation's members evaluate success?

3. "Our goal is to improve the Sunday School this year."

What does *improve* mean? Does it mean painting the rooms, recruiting more students, training teachers, selecting some different teaching materials, investing in new furniture, or providing meaningful opening exercises? Perhaps it includes several of these possibilities, but which ones?

How, Not Just What—The three goals mentioned lack sufficient specificity because they do not tell *how* action will be taken. A congregation's annual goal should include enough information to help people implement the idea and measure progress but not so much that the goal becomes wordy. Consider these revisions:

1. "Our goal is to help our members grow spiritually (what) by providing new opportunities for Bible study (how)."

2. "Our goal is to strengthen our music program (what) by adding a children's choir and an instrument ensemble and by introducing some contemporary hymns to the congregation (how)."

3. "Our goal is to equip our Sunday School teachers (what) by providing training workshops and new materials (how)."

Direction, Not Blueprint—These goals may still seem rather general in nature; however, a congregation's annual goal is always somewhat broad because it focuses on an entire aspect of ministry. Details will be added at a later point, when the goal is broken into manageable parts by boards and teams. For instance, boards working on the first goal will determine exactly what the "new opportunities for Bible study" will be, when and where groups will meet, what materials will be used, how people can be motivated to attend, who will be the leaders, what training will be needed, whether or not transportation will be provided, and so on. A congregation's annual goal points members in a clear direction with enough specificity to measure outcome; boards and teams then brainstorm to formulate all details necessary to carry out the basic plan.

Better, Not Best—The aforementioned goals are no longer ambiguous, but they are still not ready for presentation to the congregation. What else is needed? A statement of purpose must be added to show their relevance to ministry.

SECOND COMPONENT:
MINISTRY OBJECTIVE

A goal also contains a rationale. Leaders explain why they chose the action being proposed. This rationale is called the *ministry objective*. By answering the question *Why should we do it?* leaders explain to members how the proposed action is relevant to mission. Lukewarm support may result if churches write their goals merely as proposals for change and do not explain why the goals are significant.

Ministry objectives cannot be overemphasized because churches so often neglect them. These objectives are important because they serve as safeguards. A congregation can easily get caught up in activities which reflect human desire but which do not necessarily have valid purpose related to the congregation's vision for ministry. When we ask *why*, we examine our motivation and the true value of the action under consideration. If a goal has no purpose related to mission, that goal probably is not appropriate.

In addition, ministry objectives serve as motivational tools. Since goals are strategies for congregational development, they function as motivational tools that stir up the enthusiasm of members. Leaders can enlist support more readily if members understand why the goal is important in light of the congregation's vision for ministry.

The following goals are weak because they are *not* attached to ministry objectives and therefore have little power to motivate members or to stir up enthusiasm:

"We want to build a new educational wing."
"We want to begin a midweek Bible study program."
"We want to add a second pastor to the staff."
"We want to hire a full-time minister of music."
"We want to organize a senior citizens' group."
"We want to build a day-care center."

They can be strengthened by being connected to ministry objectives. How can this be done?

Ministry objectives can be written as *so-that* clauses following the action steps. For example, we can express the relevance of the youth goal mentioned previously by providing the following rationale:

> Our goal is to provide a Sunday evening program that offers Bible study, fellowship, and service opportunities for our young people *so that* they can grow in their faith in God and in their love both for one another and for other people.

By stating the purpose as spiritual growth, leaders clearly underscore their intent. They are not simply responding to parental pressure for programs; they are not competing with other churches or television; they are not trying merely to give young people something to do. Instead, they are consciously stressing their desire to help young people increase their faith in God and their love for one another and for other people.

At an earlier point in this chapter, we improved three action steps by making them more specific. However, they were not yet complete as goals because they each lacked a rationale. By adding the missing component, a ministry objective, we underscore the importance of the action steps and increase the likelihood that members will support implementation.

1. "Our goal is to help our members grow spiritually (what) by providing new opportunities for Bible study (how) *so that* **we can learn the meaning of discipleship (why)."**

2. "Our goal is to strengthen our music program (what) by adding a children's choir and an instrument ensemble and by introducing some contemporary hymns to the congregation (how) *so that* **our worship can become a dynamic witness to our faith (why)."**

3. "Our goal is to equip our Sunday School teachers (what) by providing training workshops and new materials (how) *so that* **they can communicate an excitement for God's Word (why)."**

Relevance to ministry enhances a goal's inherent power to enlist support of members. A rationale helps members understand why the proposed change is significant to the overall ministry of the congregation.

FORMULAS AND PATTERNS

The key to writing a goal is to make certain that it includes both an action step and a ministry objective. If one is not accustomed to writing goals, formulas or patterns can facilitate the process. They provide structure to ensure inclusion of essential elements, and they force us to be intentional with our communication. We will be far more likely to say what we need to say and far less likely to omit ministry objectives if we use patterns or formulas in the initial stages of writing.

Success in writing goals is not found in the format of the goals, but rather in the fact that goals are clear, specific, and complete. The following formulas and patterns should be seen as tools, not rigid guidelines. They are intended to help us clarify and organize our thoughts.

Formulas: action + purpose = goal

action step + ministry objective = goal

Fill-in-the-Blank Patterns:

Our goal is to _____ so that _____
             what and *how*   *why*

We want to _____ *(what)*
by_____ *(how)*
so that _____ *(why)*

These formulas and patterns may be helpful in facilitating the process of writing goals. They are visual forms which force leaders to express abstract ideas in concrete terms. They are not intended to limit or constrain but rather to serve as guidelines. Wide latitude is certainly permissible in the actual wording of goals.

LANGUAGE FOR GOALS

Goals should be stated in language that is clear and straightforward. Resist the temptation to add too many details and descriptive phrases. Additional explanation of ideas can always be given verbally when the goal is presented to the congregation, but the goal itself should be a succinct description of key ideas without frills or flourishes.

Formal Version—The annual goal, carefully written by the governing body, should be presented to members of the congregation in its full and complete form. A clear goal helps everyone understand the proposed action step as well as its purpose. Members at large can begin to anticipate upcoming details of the plan. Board members can use the written goal to generate discussion about how to formulate their partnership goals. As boards study the goal, they will find specific ways to contribute to the overall effort. They will suggest actions that are related to their own designated ministry areas and which can help achieve the congregation's annual goal. The complete and formal version of a goal is always used in initial stages of communication and planning.

Informal Version—Leaders can use a shortened version of the goal for promotion. Slogans on banners and bulletins can remind people of the main thrust of their ministry for the year. Examples of shortened forms of goals include the following: "Children for Christ," "Joyful Giving," "Praise God with a New Song," "God's Word in My Heart," and "Grow in God's Will."

Why spend time crafting a goal if it will be promoted in shortened form? Why not just write a slogan in the first place? A slogan cannot be a substitute for a complete goal statement because a slogan has major drawbacks. For one thing, a slogan omits crucial elements of a plan and therefore has little ability to guide detailed planning. It is a summary of the main idea, but it does not contain much information. Furthermore, a slogan does not force people to clarify their ideas or their motivation during initial decision-making stages. It can circumvent logic and allow people to meander in too many unrelated directions. A slogan or shortened form of a goal is simply a summary that can be a useful tool for publicity and visual communication through art. It is somewhat like a condensed form of a novel. It isn't as good as the original story, but it serves a purpose and communicates the key ideas quickly and well.

WRITING GOALS: THE BENEFITS

The time and effort spent in committing our goals to writing is worthwhile in many ways. Leaders benefit because their ideas can be presented clearly and with good rationale. If they continue to think in terms of specific action steps connected to ministry objectives, the congregation's organizational life will become much more fruitful. Less time will be spent on projects which do not relate to the congregation's vision for ministry. Members benefit as well because corporate life has greater meaning. They will feel joy and satisfaction in knowing that they are making significant progress toward their ultimate mission goals. Future leaders will also benefit because they can review goals of the past five to ten years and easily discern the congregation's direction in ministry. Pastors will benefit because overall ministry will have guidelines; activities will be based on purpose, not random choice. Writing goals is an important task of leadership. A carefully chosen goal that is presented effectively has power to inspire people and bring about needed change.

Goals are proposals for action that have meaning in the light of a congregation's vision for ministry. Clear statements encourage member support.

11

IMPLEMENTING CHANGE

> Once leaders formulate a goal, they must enlist widespread support of members if implementation is to be successful.

Just because leaders announce a plan or goal to the congregation does not mean members will automatically give their energy and support to it. Leaders must skillfully present and promote their ideas as well as suggest specific ways for members to help with the project. The following strategies can encourage successful implementation of goals.

PROVIDE ADEQUATE INFORMATION

Information gathering should precede the presentation of any proposal to the congregation. Leaders need to

have relevant information on hand. They should anticipate members' questions in advance and gather appropriate data to support their recommendation.

For example, if a goal is to establish a day-care center,
leaders should research the need and cost. How many
day-care facilities already exist in the area? Is there a
waiting list at these centers? Do community leaders see
day care as a need? What does it cost to build one? What
are the regulatory and insurance requirements? How
many workers will be needed in the beginning? Do we
have someone to guide the initial months of organization? Do our own members with young children have
an interest in such a facility?

If the goal is to add a staff person, leaders must gather
the necessary information. How would a second pastor
make our ministry more effective? What particular aspects of ministry would be his or her responsibility? Do
studies show that other congregations our size benefit
from adding another pastor? What steps would we
need to take to find a suitable person for the position?
How much would it cost to hire such a person? How
would the congregation raise the money? Would the
congregation need to provide housing? How soon could
we expect to find someone?

Do leaders want to make an all-out push to involve as
many members as possible in a midweek Bible study
program? If so, what programs are being considered?
What kind of time commitment is required of teachers
and participants? Is there a cost for materials? What are
the plans for training leaders? What are the projected
benefits of such an intensive program? What results
have been produced in other congregations that have
begun similar programs?

When leaders are equipped with solid answers to
questions, their proposals gain credibility. Members
feel reassured that goals are based upon sound planning and research.

Promote Through Publicity

Announcing a goal to the congregation is not enough! A goal should be promoted through every means possible. Leaders must stir up enthusiasm for the desired outcome if they are to enlist the support of other members. Banners, slogans, bulletins, newsletters, signs— any promotional tools available should be used to advertise and to keep that goal before members. Print the congregation's annual goal on the top of all meeting agendas. Provide regular progress updates in whatever forums are appropriate.

Encouragement is the key. If members understand the goal, accept it, strive to achieve it, and get regular updates on how the effort is progressing, their interest will be sustained. If a goal is simply announced at the beginning of a year and then allowed to pass into oblivion, it will have little or no effect.

Enlist Widespread Participation

Enlisting members' time and financial support requires creativity and enthusiasm. If leaders convincingly explain the goal's ministry objective and a plan for implementation, members will respond. Consider the following suggestions for achieving widespread participation.

• *Divide financial goals into segments.* An effective tactic in reaching goals is to break the objective into manageable parts. If the church needs to buy a van, break down the cost into cubic feet and encourage members to buy a cubic foot of the van. If the church needs a new roof, break the goal into numbers of shingles; ask members to buy blocks of shingles—50, 100, 500. If a new addition is to be built, ask members to purchase a square foot of the building. If rooms need to be refurbished, list items of furniture needed and the cost of each piece. If the goal is to have one or more handbell choirs, ask families to buy a bell. People often prefer to give a particular item rather than to donate money to a general fund.

• *Relate the goal or project to as many ministry areas as possible so that each organization shares responsibility for achieving the congregation's annual goal.* This is an excellent way to gain widespread support and involvement.

The following examples illustrate how each board can help to achieve the congregation's annual goal. The degree of participation will vary because some boards will relate to a specific goal more than others. The board most directly involved will supervise. Board goals, which support the annual goal, are called *partnership goals.* They can be short and do not require a ministry objective because they relate to the objective stated in the annual goal.

First Methodist Church and St. Andrew's Episcopal Church are two congregations whose boards have found ways to implement congregational goals.

FIRST METHODIST CHURCH

Vision statement: Our mission is to make disciples of all people.

Annual goal: We want to encourage members' spiritual growth by establishing small groups that will meet weekly to study, pray, and fellowship together so that we will strengthen our relationships with God and with one another.

Supervising group: Board of Congregational Life. (Since the designated responsibilities of this board most closely relate to the annual goal, Congregational Life will supervise implementation of programs.)

Partnership goals of boards—

• *Congregational Life:* To organize and support six new small groups for Bible or doctrinal study and fellowship.

- *Outreach:* To contact all visitors and invite them to visit one of the weekly small groups; to provide rides, follow-up calls, and encouragement.

- *Administration:* To work on new signs for the church and better lighting in the parking area in order to provide a safe and appealing environment for evening meetings; to begin making plans to purchase a van for those needing transportation to weekly group meetings. (There is an immediate need to pick up some older members who would like to participate but should not drive at night; as the congregation moves into more active evangelism, there will also be a need to pick up new people who need transportation.)

- *Education:* To assist the pastor in training small group leaders and to select study materials that could guide the Bible study.

- *Service:* To recruit leaders for these new endeavors and to help new members find a place to serve once they join the church.

Note: Boards may contribute in more than one way to accomplish the annual goal.

ST. ANDREW'S EPISCOPAL CHURCH

Vision statement: Our purpose is to show and proclaim the love of Jesus to everyone we encounter.

Annual goal: We want to make our worship a dynamic celebration of the Gospel by using creative formats and activities so that more people will attend, hear God's Word, and receive the Sacraments.

Supervising group: Board of Worship

Partnership goals of boards—

- *Worship:* To make innovative changes in the worship service so that it will appeal to a variety of people.

(Ideas include a new bulletin format that is user-friendly, the addition of a children's choir, incorporation of lay prayers in the service, use of contemporary hymns and children's sermons, and welcoming activities for newcomers.)

- *Education:* To teach children the meaning of worship and find ways for them to participate. (Ideas include having children design bulletin covers occasionally, learn hymns during their Sunday School openings, write prayers for use in the worship service, and sit together in church as classes once every quarter.)

- *Administration:* To improve or replace the sound system.

- *Outreach:* To provide weekly news releases to the local newspaper and to make personal contact with all visitors within five days.

- *Service:* To locate members who are interested in assisting with many new aspects of worship. (Ideas include supplying a list of potential children for the choir, assisting in locating a choir director and persons interested in making banners, and arranging rides for people who need transportation in order to attend the worship services.)

- *Congregational Life:* To form a youth choir, begin integrating youth as ushers and lay readers, and provide monthly fellowship dinners after worship.

Three years later St. Andrew's is ready to initiate an aggressive evangelism program. The vision statement remains the same, of course. However, the annual goal changes: "Our goal is to train members for outreach by providing classes that will teach them how to witness so that they can tell others about God's love."

Supervising group: Outreach Board

Partnership goals of boards—

- *Outreach:* To help members develop witnessing skills.

- *Worship:* To emphasize in our services the theme of witnessing in vocational and other daily settings.

- *Education:* To make plans for special classes designed to help newcomers become acquainted with the church and grow in their faith.

- *Administration:* To repaint community signs that advertise the church's presence and location; to make the building accessible to the handicapped.

- *Congregational Life:* To plan special get-acquainted events for newcomers.

- *Service:* To recruit people to teach the classes on witnessing; to assist new members in finding places to serve once they join the church.

All of these annual thrusts still point toward the parish's shared vision. Each organization still has its ongoing tasks, but in addition, it adopts an initiative that contributes to the congregation's annual goal. As organizations work on various aspects of the common goal, their united efforts generate a sense of team work and team success.

DEVELOP LONG-RANGE PLANS

Major goals can be divided into incremental steps that can be taken over the course of several years. Long-range plans give congregations a clear sense of direction and suggest an orderly progression of effort.

For example, one congregation, whose vision statement targeted evangelism, decided to concentrate on developing congregational life for a period of three years, followed by outreach the next two years. Leaders broke the five-year plan into two parts. Phase I focused on worship, study, and stewardship; goals were formulated to create change in each of those ministry areas. Phase II focused on training members in evangelism and actual witness in their everyday lives and vocations. This five-year plan was evaluated at the end of each year to note progress and make adjustments.

Another congregation, whose vision statement focused upon discipleship, decided to formulate goals based upon the various disciplines of faith. They chose focus areas and then wrote goals that were ministry objectives with specific ideas for change. Their five-year plan focused upon prayer and study, worship, stewardship, witness, and working for justice.

Yet another congregation, whose vision statement focused on embodying God's love, made a five-year plan geared toward helping people experience and express the love of God. Their goals related to knowing God's love—as individuals, as families, and as members of the church—and to sharing God's love with their city, and finally, with the world community.

Long-range planning helps people see how current goals pertain to the overall progression toward a bigger objective. Looking ahead builds excitement. With each year the momentum builds, and members can rejoice in accomplishment. Creative possibilities for long-range planning are unlimited.

If goals are to become reality, they must be understood and accepted. Implementation strategies include gathering pertinent background information, soliciting widespread involvement by individuals and groups, and developing long-range plans.

12

CELEBRATION

Celebration and thanksgiving energize us for service. Congregations need to develop a celebrative culture in their midst as they recognize God's blessings and acknowledge the gifts of members who contribute to ministry.

Steps chiseled in solid rock and winding trails lead thousands of visitors annually on a descent into a wonderland of color and fragrance. Butchart Gardens, once an abandoned rock quarry on Vancouver Island, now flourishes as a lush garden with towering trees and a vast array of blooming flowers and bushes. How did an old rock quarry become a dazzling garden?

Decades ago, a new owner conceived the idea of transforming the old quarry into a magnificent garden. Year after year, he hauled dirt down steep pathways, filling the vast crater with soil one wheelbarrow load at a time. Gradually, the garden began to take shape. As he filled each corner with life-sustaining soil, he planted tiny seeds. Eventually, the entire quarry sprang to life.

Did the man realize when he began that the task would be so great? Did he ever get discouraged? What gave him energy to continue?

He no doubt had a vision in his heart that guided his hand. Perhaps he pictured a time when red, yellow, pink, blue, purple, and every shade of green would cover the cliffs and delight the eye. He must have gazed with pleasure at the beds of flowers he had already completed, those once empty spots now resplendent with new life. The small successes no doubt spurred him on as he labored to develop a barren area more vast than his eye could see. And so it was! Wheelbarrow by wheelbarrow, one load at a time, the ugliness was transformed by the gardener into indescribable beauty.

What does quarry restoration have to do with church work? Both are formidable challenges that require commitment and perseverance. The gardener, weary from pushing his wheelbarrow up and down the quarry trails, must have wondered if his many trips were a waste of time—inadequate for such a huge undertaking. Yet, his dream and his energy bore fruit. We, too, sometimes wonder if our efforts in the church are sufficient for the task. How can we possibly do what God asks? Do our small efforts have any significance? Like the gardener, we need to pause from time to time to rest, to dream, and to rejoice in progress. Our energy and excitement for ministry will only be sustained if we stop periodically to celebrate the steps we have already taken.

THE VALUE OF CELEBRATION

We may agree that celebration is important, but because life is hectic, we are sometimes tempted to neglect it in order to accomplish more urgent tasks of ministry.

Celebration, however, is not an optional activity. Expressing our appreciation for God's blessings and the contributions of those who serve is a crucial element of corporate life for several important reasons.

First of all, celebration reinforces our identity and calling as God's people. Thankfulness and celebration have ancient roots. In Biblical history, festivals and feast days were important occasions when people gave thanks for God's provision, guidance, protection, and deliverance. The Hebrews built altars, gave offerings, made sacrifices, prayed, sang, and danced. They also recounted stories of past blessings to remind everyone that God is faithful and almighty. Their celebrations gave them hope and courage to persevere. Celebrations were an integral part of corporate life because they reminded people that they were blessed in order that they might be a blessing to others.

Celebration is no less important today. Pausing to give thanks reminds us of our identity as God's people and helps us remain focused on our mission. Whenever we pray, sing, dance, give special offerings, tell stories of God's work in our lives, or do any number of other celebrative activities, we, like our ancestors, underscore our reliance on God and strengthen our bond with one another.

Celebration also lifts our spirits by encouraging us. This is especially important in the realm of church work. Why? Because our work is ongoing in nature. In truth, God's work is never finished. There is never a time when the faithful can sit down and say, "Well, we've finished our job. There's nothing more for us to do." Works of compassion, teaching, sharing, uplifting, forgiving, nurturing, and witnessing are continually needed. Therefore, if we mentally associate celebration with the idea of work completion and postpone it indefinitely, we may give up long before we reach our goals. Rather, we should pause often to celebrate what we have already accomplished so that we can be encouraged by our progress and motivated to continue.

It is not only all right to feel good about accomplishing Kingdom work, but it is essential. If church members cannot feel a sense of accomplishment, they get discouraged and stop trying. Celebrations draw members closer to each other in thankfulness for success and in anticipation of further progress.

Major Congregational Milestones

Anniversaries, dedications, and conclusions of special campaigns or projects have long been recognized as times for special celebration in congregational life. These milestones represent major achievements. As such, they are usually acknowledged with elaborate festivities requiring months of planning and effort. Like rallies, they stir up excitement and energize participants.

There are countless ways to celebrate major milestones. What is important is that imagination and creativity be allowed to shape planning. Bright colors, flowers, balloons, unique table arrangements, photo displays, crepe-paper streamers—all express excitement. Speakers can infuse the group with enthusiasm as they underscore the significance of an occasion. Presentations of history using anecdotes and old photos are appropriate for anniversary celebrations. Entertainment such as music, crafts, skits, storytelling, or role playing is always enjoyable and appropriate to celebration. Potluck or catered dinners, picnics, group singing, and games are all activities that are interactive and encourage people to enjoy one another.

Congregational celebration provides a wonderful opportunity to highlight ministry objectives. Although major events generate happiness in and of themselves with their activities, fun, and fellowship, they can have even greater impact if members see the long-term significance of the event as it relates to their goals. For example, we may celebrate a church anniversary for such basic and simple reasons as these: "We are proud to be an old church; we enjoy each other; we think our future is bright." However, the occasion takes on a deeper significance if planners use the opportunity to remind members of God's faithfulness throughout their history and of the dedication of those who, despite adversity, struggled to build a congregation. Stories of the past inspire members to renew their own commitment to accomplishing their vision for ministry. An anniversary thus becomes much more than just a pleasant day; it becomes a day that lifts our spirits and affirms the importance of our work.

SMALL TRIUMPHS

If we celebrate only on rare and special occasions, we minimize daily victories that occur on a small scale but which are equally important. Celebration does not always have to be a massive endeavor. Small celebrations serve to lift spirits and encourage people as they face the ongoing challenges of ministry. They might be called *pause points*—occasions to stop, reflect, change the routine, and express gratitude. Small celebrations are especially appropriate in organizational work as a means of promoting group spirit and acknowledging progress. They add variety to routines and do not require heavy expenditures of time or money. We can use small celebrative moments to thank individuals, to note completion of a project, or simply to provide an atmosphere in which participants can share the joy of being part of God's family. Boards, teams, the governing body, support groups, or any church organization can plan such moments from time to time to encourage members.

Celebrative touches can be as simple as balloons, flowers, a gift, special refreshments, or the sharing of humorous anecdotes related to accomplishing a goal.

The idea is that we need to break our routines for celebration; variety in our work patterns adds excitement and interest. Simply changing the meeting place from the church to a member's home or to a restaurant can perk up the spirits of members. Other change-of-pace ideas include guest speakers, visits to other churches, videos, picnics, games, and skits. Creative ideas can help us get to know one another better and build group spirit.

Celebration helps us cultivate an attitude of appreciation and thanksgiving in the congregation. As we learn to discern small signs of progress, we become more positive in outlook and more willing to contribute time and effort to ministry.

CELEBRATING FAITHFUL SERVICE

Why should we thank those who serve? The old saying "Success breeds success" suggests that people are encouraged by positive experiences. Members who feel their efforts are worthwhile are much more likely to remain active and excited. When we pause to acknowledge people's efforts and to note signs of progress, we usually build momentum for achieving our goals. Furthermore, focusing on members' contributions helps everyone realize that progress is not automatic. Forward movement in ministry only happens when people are sensitive to God's leading and generous in their expenditure of effort.

Congregations need to be intentional about communicating appreciation lest members take faithful service for granted. Public recognition of workers increases awareness of the variety of tasks involved in the congregation's overall ministry. Public expressions of gratitude should be sincere, carefully prepared, personalized to the degree possible, appropriate, and related to ministry objectives so that members understand the significance of the contribution. The efforts of individuals or groups are important in the context of helping us achieve our goals. We don't celebrate just because a person has filled a position or because another year has passed. Celebrations should focus on how certain individuals have successfully moved us toward achieving our ministry goals. Again, the idea is that activity be purposeful. Busyness in and of itself is not necessarily something to celebrate. Celebrations are opportunities to remind people that they are headed in a particular direction. They work together because their work has purpose.

THANKING GROUPS

How can we thank groups of people, such as officers, choir members, teachers, and so on? If recognition is done within the context of the worship service, one way to make a group thank-you meaningful is to incorporate thoughtfully worded statements that describe the work of those honored. A photo display in the fellowship area could give further evidence of the scope of the group's activity. Having Bible School children sing a thank-you to their teachers is another example of how to make appreciation memorable. A congregation might personalize its thank-you to Sunday School teachers by soliciting letters of appreciation from parents or by having all of the children come forward, gather around the teachers, and present a large handmade card with drawings and words of appreciation. A meaningful presentation not only affirms those who serve but also emphasizes the nature and significance of their contribution.

If recognition is done outside the context of worship, greater flexibility is possible. Suppose, for example, that your congregation usually thanks Sunday School teachers at a potluck dinner. Instead of giving each teacher a certificate of appreciation after the dinner, why not make, throughout the year, a videotape that would show the teachers in action? A student or parent representing each class could make a short comment about the teacher; it could be a funny anecdote or a loving tribute. If the congregation is trying to build interest in education and promote its importance, this event should be done in the context of a congregational fellowship gathering so that everyone can be exposed to the video and stories, not just the Sunday School staff. Such a celebration would be fun! It would be personal in that teachers would not be lumped together for recognition; each would be recognized for his or her unique contribution.

Outgoing officers of the congregation are also usually thanked as a group at the end of their tenure. Sometimes it is appropriate to personalize appreciation with special remarks.

> We want to thank you, John, for your wisdom in guiding us through the decision to call a second pastor. You listened to our debate, and you promptly provided us with helpful information. You had us all laughing at times when we might otherwise have been arguing. We especially remember when you . . . . Without your wisdom and careful planning, we would not have reached this point. Thank you for the time you have given, for your prayers, and for your excellent leadership as president of our congregation! You have made a difference in our life together!

Lavish thank-you's are not necessary, but creative and thoughtful expressions of gratitude can help everyone grow in their understanding and appreciation of the work that was done.

THANKING INDIVIDUALS

How can we thank individuals whose work has been particularly noteworthy? Perhaps we want to thank a pastor, a choir director, or someone who has served in a specific capacity with unusual dedication. If the person has served for many years, perhaps a "This Is Your Life" presentation could be used. Original skits, song parodies, photos, and spoken tributes and anecdotes could, for example, honor a retiring pastor. An organist who has served for many years might be honored as members recount the musical history of the church. Undoubtedly, there would be many humorous stories to share. Perhaps someone served as head of a building project and spent countless hours with details and supervision. A reception honoring that person could be held following the worship service. The pastor or president of the congregation could express appreciation on behalf of all the members. Several co-workers could share details about the person's leadership as the project developed.

Again, connecting the celebration to the congregation's progress in ministry gives greater depth and significance to the occasion. Members need to acknowledge not only the person's work but also why the work was important. Even if members thank the individual profusely and give a gift, if there is no recognition of why that person's work was significant to ministry, the event will fall short in terms of impact.

Celebrating Heritage

Telling our history should be a regular and important ingredient of congregational life. When congregations remember their past—events, key persons, turning points—they allow their history to influence their thinking and identity. Slides, scrapbooks, videos, taped interviews, and displays all contribute to a congregation's sense of identity and progress. Reflecting on the past can inspire us to give thanks for the faith of all who have made ministry today a reality. Looking back also gives us courage to move forward boldly in new directions.

Interweaving past, present, and future is a wonderful way to build fervor. A heritage-and-vision event can launch a building campaign or new program by giving added meaning to the occasion. A focus on heritage causes members to reflect on past achievements with thanksgiving and pride; they see the relevance of present goals to their vision for ministry as it has been unfolding over the years, and they are inspired to move forward. Celebration that looks at the whole scope of a congregation's activity helps members realize that God's work is ongoing in nature and that they are in partnership with Him and with each other to share the Gospel and advance the Kingdom.

AD HOC PLANNING TEAMS

Who should plan congregational celebrations? We usually rely on our leaders to plan celebrations. Why? Because they often seem to know what to do and how to do it better than those who are less active. The drawback, however, is obvious: Leaders who are already spending long hours in ministry may not wish to take on additional responsibilities. They may agree that celebration is important but may not have additional time to commit to planning.

One solution is to assemble an ad hoc team to organize a celebration so that leaders do not feel an additional burden of responsibility. Most congregations are veritable treasure chests of creativity. The experiences and ideas of people merely need to be tapped. Those who are less heavily involved may welcome a chance to show appreciation to those who spend countless hours in their behalf. The point is that instead of requiring leaders to plan congregational celebrations, we can solicit the help of those who are less actively involved but who are willing to work with short-term projects. Leaders may need to initiate plans and offer suggestions, but others can certainly plan the details.

MAKING IT HAPPEN

Organizational life in the church depends upon mobilizing members for ministry. Leaders are constantly challenged to find ways to motivate members, to involve them meaningfully, and to encourage them. Because the scope of activity is so broad, members often have a fragmented view of what is being accomplished. They may judge congregational vitality by what is going on in a single area of ministry and thus become discouraged. Celebration is an opportunity to broaden perspectives, to give members a more complete view of the congregation's activity. It also enables us to see that our work is bearing fruit. Thus, celebration is an important strategy for maintaining organizational vitality. It can make a vast difference in the attitudes of members and in their willingness to participate in ministry. We need to thank God for his guidance and blessing, to acknowledge progress in ministry, and to thank both volunteers and paid staff for their dedication.

Celebrations are essential to a congregation's life because they remind us that we are a family of God working together for common goals. Celebrations are pause points—times to pause in our work in order to rest, reflect, and rejoice.

LEADERSHIP

SECTION THREE

Improving Your Skills

Anyone can be a leader! True? Perhaps. Certainly anyone who is willing to assume responsibility for a committee or a ministry task could be designated a leader. But if accepting a job invitation is all it takes to make someone a leader, why do so many willing persons flounder as leaders of church committees?

Unfortunately, the church has long operated on the faulty premise that all adults have an inherent grasp of leadership skills. We confer titles of responsibility upon people and expect them to have instant expertise. Although some laypersons are capable leaders because of past experience, many others have never been actively involved in positions that required leadership. If a congregation focuses simply on filling positions and does not recognize the need to provide leadership training, its ministry may suffer.

Successful ministry is most likely to occur when those who lead have clear job descriptions and at least some training in making agendas, conducting meetings, leading discussions, resolving conflicts, delegating, keeping records, and planning ahead. Once new leaders understand basic how-to's, they become more confident, enthusiastic, and effective.

Training is important for potential leaders in any environment, but it is especially important in the church because the environment is unique. Maintaining harmony becomes a primary goal for most church leaders because they believe the church is supposed to be a loving and peaceful place at all times. We underestimate the inhibiting effect of trying to avoid conflict while working with our fellow believers. We may feel a tension between our desire for pleasant relationships and our desire to accomplish ministry. As leaders, we worry that someone on the committee may be offended along the way and leave the church. Such a possibility lurks in the background and often causes us to curtail use of important leadership skills. Consequently, we become overly cautious and are hesitant to initiate change before we are certain of widespread support.

Not only are co-workers our friends, but they, too, are volunteers who freely give their time and energy to ministry. How much can we expect of them? How far can we go in requiring accountability? How do we exercise authority without being offensive? Leaders need preparation that will help them anticipate problems and avoid unnecessary frustration.

Leadership training is not an option! It is a necessity if the church is to meet the challenges of ministry to a troubled world and if the church is dedicated to improving the quality of experience for volunteers. Most people accept their leadership responsibilities because they believe the work is important and because they are willing to help. The church's task is to provide them with tools to increase their effectiveness. They need both education about working in the church environment and training in leadership skills.

Organizations take on new vitality when the church actively stresses the importance of leadership by providing high-quality training. With a clearer vision of how to proceed, leaders will gain confidence and produce better results.

Perhaps you have accepted a leadership position in your church and are looking for some practical help and training. The following chapters will provide useful suggestions and tips for increasing your effectiveness and will help you serve in the Body of Christ with confidence!

13

LEADERSHIP STYLES

Our service in the church becomes more effective
when we recognize our own style of leadership
and match it to both the job and situation.

Being designated a leader does not confer skill or guarantee good results. Sometimes capable people are un-
successful in leadership positions due to a simple and
fundamental problem: Their style of leading is not suited
to the situation.

Leadership style is an outgrowth of our attitudes,
personality, and experiences. Our style is expressed in
how we use time, work with others, make plans, and
conduct meetings. It also is reflective of our priorities.
Some of us are primarily task oriented while others of
us are relationship oriented. Discovering our leadership style and understanding its implications can help
us serve where we will produce maximum results.

Volumes of material have been written on leadership styles. The purpose of this chapter is not to give a comprehensive analysis of the subject, but to provide a simple explanation that can help you identify your own style.

In his book *Friedman's Fables*, Rabbi Edwin Friedman includes a humorous parable called "Net Results."[1] The parable is about single-minded people who go to absurd lengths to achieve success despite signals of disinterest from those whose cooperation is necessary. The following paraphrase relates the story:

> A man named Harry wanted to improve his wife's tennis game (not that *she* cared very much about the sport). He had already given her lessons, books, and new shoes, but her game never seemed to improve. One lovely morning he took his reluctant wife to the court. He determined once and for all to overcome all obstacles and help her to succeed. When they arrived at the tennis court, he reviewed many of the pointers he had mentioned the night before. He reminded her how to hold the racket, how to position her feet, and so on. Then he hurried to his side of the court and prepared to serve. "Ready, dear?" he asked. She nodded. He served, but the ball zipped past her. "What happened?" he asked. "I wasn't ready," she replied. Undaunted, he served again.
>
> They continued to play. Sometimes she hit the ball, but it usually would hit the net or go over his head. He tried to encourage her, but once she responded, "Don't you think we should paint the house this summer?"
>
> Harry kept running over to her side to suggest some special technique or to demonstrate a proper position. Then he would run back to his side and serve again. Once, he even tried holding her racquet with her, lobbing the ball, and running back over to his side to return it, but nothing seemed to improve her game. "Don't you want to play?" he asked. "It was your idea," she replied.

[1]*Friedman's Fables* by Edwin H. Friedman, copyright 1990 by Guilford Publications: New York. Adapted and reprinted by permission of the author.

Utterly frustrated, he finally figured out what to do. He wiped the sweat from his head and served a very high lob. Quickly he ran over to her side of the court so he could be there himself when the ball came down. He  was ready for the return. He hit the ball up in the air with all his might and dashed to his own side once again to return the ball. And so the match continued. From that time on, Harry never again let the ball bounce twice on her side of the court.

Although Harry's story is an exaggeration, the point is not far-fetched. In the parable, Harry has a clear goal in mind—to teach his wife how to play tennis. So far, so good. That goal, however, requires his wife's cooperation, and unfortunately, she doesn't concentrate or want to try. Harry is so intent upon accomplishing his goal that he is oblivious to signs of his wife's disinterest. Not even her exasperated reminder that the whole thing was his idea in the first place brings him to an awareness that his goal is futile. He is completely focused on the task he wants to accomplish.

Does Harry achieve his goal? In his zeal to teach his wife to play tennis, he ends up playing the game for her. He uses her space to play his game. Church leaders often do a similar thing. In their zeal to get a job done, they sometimes become oblivious to signals of disinterest or resistance in co-workers. Determined to accomplish their goals, they end up doing the job alone. What should have been a team effort becomes a one-person show.

RECOGNIZING YOUR LEADERSHIP STYLE

Our personality traits affect the way we lead; they cause us to develop certain ways of handling responsibility and relating to others. If we understand why some situations produce frustration for us while others bring satisfaction, we can begin to seek jobs for which we are well suited. Discovering and understanding our own personality strengths and weaknesses will enable us to serve in leadership settings where we can be more effective and derive a greater sense of personal fulfillment.

Each style described below has its strengths and drawbacks. Descriptions are exaggerated for the purpose of identification. Most of us fall somewhere in between the extremes, but it is helpful to recognize which style is dominant in us. Which description best identifies your style?

TASK ORIENTATION

You find your main satisfaction in getting things done. You gain more self-esteem from concrete achievement than from the opinions others may have of you. You work best in a formal, structured setting in which expectations are clear. You use agendas because they help maintain group focus. You plan, organize, set goals, and are always aware of time requirements. You welcome input from others as long as their thoughts are productive and move the group toward accomplishing the goal. Your major contribution is the ability to organize and get a job done efficiently.

Difficulties of this leadership style spring from your single-mindedness. You tend to be annoyed by wasted time, idle chatter, and irresponsible people. Work is important to you; you have little patience with those who let you down. In fact, when others disappoint you by failing to carry out their responsibilities, your frustration with their poor job performance may translate into a personal dislike for them. You tend to be impatient with those who are easily distracted because one of your strengths is an ability to concentrate. You view time as valuable and meetings as opportunities for work. In the extreme, you are like Harry. You will get the job done even if you have to do it yourself!

RELATIONSHIP ORIENTATION

You place a high priority on your relationships with other people. Your self-esteem greatly depends on how other people regard you. You are sensitive to what group members feel and seek to please them with warmth and tact. You enjoy problem solving, being creative, and helping a group generate ideas, but you try to avoid actions that might cause hurt feelings. You value individual opinions and seek to provide a comfortable environment where they can be expressed. The process tends to be more important to you than the end result. You are adept at facilitating group interaction and encouraging relationship building. Your communication skills and sensitivity promote harmony and solidarity.

Disadvantages arise from your reluctance to be assertive under stress and your lack of patience with organizational details. You tend to avoid constraints because they diminish flexibility. Fellowship and understanding among members usually takes precedence over making decisions in the allotted time; you want to get the job done but not at the expense of relationships. Urgency is a factor that usually hinders your effectiveness and causes anxiety because you are reluctant to prod others or adhere to deadlines.

SATISFACTION AND SUCCESS

As a task-oriented person, you evaluate success at the end of a meeting in this way: "Did we accomplish what we set out to do?" Your satisfaction is less contingent on group support and warm feelings than on decisive action.

As a relationship-oriented person, you evaluate success at the end of a meeting in this way: "Did the members relate well to each other? Did they all have a chance to speak and share their thoughts?" You are not

overly distressed by lack of concrete achievement if the
members had meaningful interaction.[2]

FINDING YOUR NICHE

Churches offer a wide variety of ways to serve. Some
jobs are more suited to task-oriented persons; other jobs
require the skills of those who are relationship oriented.
Since service opportunities abound, you need to consider matching your style to the job. You can be most
effective serving in areas of church leadership that require the skills you actually have and enjoy using. How
easy it would be if the church could divide its service
opportunities into clear categories: one group of jobs
would require task-oriented leaders; the other would
require relationship-oriented leaders. This is not possible, of course, since few jobs fall into a single category.
It is possible, however, to use a general guideline when
considering a leadership position: Serve where you are
challenged and have skills that match the job priorities.

For example, suppose you are predominantly a
relationship-oriented person. You enjoy getting to know
people, problem solving, creative thinking, discussion,
and motivating others to work together. Your excitement and energy come from meaningful interaction.
You work best in an atmosphere of freedom and flexibility. What positions would be best for you?

Work where you can be a catalyst for interaction.
Choose settings in which your verbal skills can have a
major impact. Possibilities include leading study groups,
support groups, and training sessions for volunteers, as
well as handling personnel, recruiting helpers, or promoting ideas. You could also work with evangelism or
ministry efforts involving home visitation because you
enjoy meeting people. You probably should avoid jobs

---

[2]These ideas are adapted from publications by Fred E. Fiedler and Martin M.
Chemers. Further information can be found in their book *Improving Leadership Effectiveness*, published by Wiley Press, New York, 1984.

that involve solitude, routine, an emphasis on planning, administrative detail, or deadlines.

If, on the other hand, you are predominantly task oriented, you should serve in positions that require structure, scheduling, and organization. Your skills are needed in any position requiring attention to details. If you like the challenge of working with a group, you can serve as chair of a board or team, director of parish education, or head of a building program. These are examples of service that would allow you to use the full range of your skills in anticipating problems, planning, making agendas, overseeing progress, and taking action.

If you happen to be an extremely task-oriented person, you may find group work altogether too frustrating; you simply cannot tolerate it when others waste time or do not fulfill their responsibilities. In such a case, you may need to find a position (such as financial secretary or librarian) that allows you to work independently. Another solution would be to serve where you can choose your co-workers, people who also are task oriented.

If your role is well suited to your leadership style, not only will the church benefit, but you will have a much greater sense of satisfaction in serving. We have all seen the results of placing square pegs in round holes: asking relationship-oriented leaders to do jobs that require a high degree of structure and attention to detail or asking task-oriented leaders to handle situations that require highly developed communication or motivational skills.

Does this mean that you should avoid any job for which you are not especially suited? No, indeed. You simply need to anticipate that such a job may be more frustrating and difficult for you; the results may still be worth the effort.

If you are asked to serve in a leadership position that interests you but does not match your leadership style,

effort," he says. Sadly, there is no job description, no record of what has been done in the past, no committee, and meager resources. He must begin from square one.

Because he is eager to get started, his first instinct is to figure things out himself. He would like to study successful programs in other churches, put together a plan to present to his board when it convenes, and encourage quick implementation of his ideas. He could assign everyone a task and get the plan in motion at the initial meeting. This idea seems like the expedient solution. If he does all of the work in advance, he will save valuable group time.

A second alternative is to go to the first meeting with no plans at all and involve members in the slower process of creating a plan together. If they develop ideas themselves, they will probably be more enthusiastic about implementation, but they will also waste valuable time at the outset of the year. What should he do?

He evaluates the merits of both alternatives and chooses a compromise strategy. He begins to recruit interested persons for his board while at the same time reading and talking to friends about evangelism efforts in other churches. When the day of the initial meeting approaches, he does not yet have a clear program in mind, but he has several preliminary ideas and key questions to stimulate group discussion. By engaging his members in active dialogue, he hopes to use their collective experiences and wisdom to begin working out a plan for the year. They may use his ideas, or they may develop other options themselves, but his preliminary research will jump-start their creative thinking.

To a large degree, his success will depend on how well he continues to blend relational skills with his own drive to accomplish the task. Group work requires management of time and task but also the ability to involve others in planning and implementation.

AVOIDING BURNOUT

The democratic process—necessary in volunteer organizations—is slower than autocratic management.

People who have high personal efficiency standards may have a hard time adjusting to slower processes associated with church committees. If you are a task-oriented leader, you may be especially susceptible to burnout because of your high expectations. You may become discouraged and frustrated with co-workers who do not follow through with their responsibilities, and you may think you must resort to doing jobs that do not require you to rely on anyone else.

One way to avoid this situation is to eliminate from the beginning some of the potential for disappointment. That is, choose co-workers who are dependable and eager to get the job done. As you recruit people, tell them at the outset that you intend to have a *working* board or team—one in which individuals will spend time working on assignments between meetings. (Some church committees meet monthly for discussion but seldom require individual members to work during the interim.) Describe your expectations of sharing the workload so that there will be no misconceptions. Then learn to delegate effectively.

Whether you are task oriented or relationship oriented, it is important to always keep in mind your own strengths and limitations when assuming a leadership role. Consider the job requirements and whether or not you will have adequate help. After you begin work, continually anticipate your needs and take steps to avoid pitfalls by planning carefully, by recruiting more help when necessary, and by skillfully leading those with whom you work. In this way, you will be more successful in avoiding burnout.

Remember the analogy of bobbing for apples? Apples are the dreams and goals of the church. The playmates or guests at the party are volunteers in the church who bring expectancy and excitement to the gathering. The tub, the room, the house—all constitute the setting—the environment in which the activity will take place. Goals,

 people, location—but *who* will get things going? *Who* will initiate the action and direct the festivities? LEADERS! Leaders are hosts for the party. Translated into congregational life, leaders instigate the action. They make it happen. They provide a context in which all can participate in achieving a goal. *How* they lead will determine the outcome.

Understanding and appreciating your own leadership style can enable you to serve wisely. As a Christian leader, you face exciting challenges in a world which desperately needs to hear the Gospel. Serve where you can express your own giftedness. Paul's analogy of the Church as the Body of Christ indicates that each member has a specific function—"many parts, but one body" (I Corinthians 12). We serve most effectively when we understand our own unique abilities and respect those of others in our fellowship.

Understanding the differences between task-oriented leadership and relationship-oriented leadership can help us serve more effectively. These styles are not mutually exclusive; both are appropriate and necessary for effective leadership.

14

AGENDAS

> An agenda is a creative tool that promotes order, balance, and efficiency in meetings. Submitting the agenda to participants for amendment or approval invites them to share their use of time responsibly.

A major challenge in organizational work is that of making time spent in meetings as productive as possible. A complaint in Christian circles is that committee meetings are tiresome and, to use Shakespeare's phrase, "much ado about nothing." Leaders have an obligation to be good stewards of time given by co-workers. Their goal should be to make meetings fruitful. An agenda can be an effective tool in this regard because it allows the leader to influence both the content and the time flow of a meeting. A carefully planned agenda encourages productivity in several important ways:

1. *An agenda promotes orderly conduct of business.* In creating an agenda, a leader prioritizes topics by including major concerns and by eliminating items that do not warrant committee time. He or she thus takes into account the urgency of certain tasks and places them high on the agenda for consideration early in the meeting.

2. *An agenda promotes efficient use of time.* By clearly defining the purpose of the meeting, an agenda deters pointless digression into unrelated topics. Meetings sometimes deteriorate when participants bring up unexpected subjects. An agenda also discourages limitless discussion of a single item because members can see that additional items remain and realize that the meeting must move forward. One method of helping members focus and agree on use of time is to invite their acceptance or amendment of the agenda at the beginning of the meeting. Once members agree to the plan, all discussion should relate to items on the approved agenda.

3. *An agenda provides balance by including all necessary ingredients.* Certain processes may never occur unless they are deemed important enough to be scheduled on the agenda. For example, such activities as evaluating, long-range planning, and creative thinking are often pushed aside in favor of more pressing matters. Intentional inclusion allows them to become a regular and meaningful part of meetings.

Trial and Error

Does an agenda guarantee a successful meeting? No! Not all agendas produce good results. Consider the following examples of good intentions that resulted in failure.

> *Katherine:* My first meeting was a disaster. I wanted to be well prepared, so I wrote a long, detailed agenda of

items for discussion. I guess I tried to accomplish too much in one session. They really like to talk! I didn't want to offend anyone, so I didn't intervene when they began sharing personal experiences. We only covered four of the twelve items I had included. I went home frustrated and aware that we had accomplished far less than I had hoped.

Antonio: I had a great idea for my first meeting! I added a time limit beside each item on my agenda. I knew that people tended to get into lengthy debates, so I put the number of minutes allowed for discussion in clear print right beside each topic on the agenda. My plan was a failure though. My committee members were frustrated because they couldn't program their input to fit within my time frame. They had to make rushed decisions and seemed dissatisfied.

Charlie: I just use the same plan every time. It saves me time to just list the usual things—minutes, reports, old business, new business, and announcements—but people usually seem kind of bored. Members don't come regularly and never pay much attention to the agenda. I guess they already know what it says.

We have probably all fumbled at times in our attempts to work out a good plan for a meeting. We sometimes overplan by including too many items, or we underestimate the amount of time needed for discussion, but we can learn from our mistakes. We can make adjustments in our planning until we understand how to do it well.

Agendas are creative tools; therefore, they have no rigid format. They will be different for every meeting in order to reflect changing concerns and needs. They may include planning, evaluation, assignment of responsibilities, decision making, long-range planning, reporting, or announcements. No agenda needs all of these elements at once, but they are all appropriate and should appear in the course of a year.

MEETING CHECKLIST

1. *Clarify the purpose of the meeting.* Every meeting should be purpose oriented. The people gathered may consider various topics, but the main purpose should be written on the agenda and underscored verbally at the beginning of the meeting. The leader might say, for example, "Our main purpose this evening is to plan our Rally Day program, but we also want to do preliminary planning for teacher recruitment." Knowing the purpose helps members focus their thoughts.

2. *Consider priority items during the early part of a meeting.* Attention of members is usually at its peak during the first half of a meeting. Therefore, if there are issues that demand vigorous discussion or difficult decision making, those should be placed on the first part of the agenda so that they can be given optimum attention.

Of course, one reality of life is that most meetings have stragglers, people who arrive late. These persons need time to make a transition from the world outside to the business at hand. They also need to hear information pertinent to the priority items, which they may have missed by coming late. A leader can avoid the need to repeat information for stragglers by placing priority items 15 to 20 minutes into the meeting rather than at the absolute beginning.

3. *Include change-of-pace items to sustain interest and involvement.* Interspersing short, less strenuous items among ones that require heavy deliberation gives members a chance to ease up mentally. If there is a succession of difficult matters, members tend to become tired and lose their ability to concentrate.

4. *Fit agenda items into the time period agreed upon by committee members.* Leaders are responsible for governing the time flow. They should keep the meeting moving at a comfortable rate, minimizing digression. If the

leader respects time covenants, participants will not have to tiptoe out with guilty demeanor when the meeting runs far beyond its designated conclusion time. Furthermore, if members have an agenda, they can see how many items need to be considered during the meeting and will be less likely to sidetrack progress.

Granted, some circumstances warrant departure from the usual routines, but ordinarily the leader should confine the meeting to a reasonable period of time so that people can plan accordingly. If an emergency arises requiring a longer meeting, the leader should contact group members in advance to apprise them of the situation.

5. *Minimize reading of lengthy reports.* Long, written reports have a deadening effect if read aloud in meetings. Highlighting or summarizing is generally preferable to reading lengthy reports in their entirety. Whenever possible, mail reports to members in advance.

6. *Provide ample time for individual input.* Generally speaking, people feel that their time is spent in a worthwhile manner if they have ample chance to share ideas and make decisions.

Sometimes leaders try to save the time and energy of group members by doing all of the planning themselves, prior to the meeting. They present their plan and are often surprised by a lack of positive response. Making detailed plans or decisions outside of the committee, even if done with good intentions, often fails in the long run because committee members feel used and unimportant; they lack excitement because they have had no creative input in planning. The drawbacks of such action usually outweigh any benefits. Discussion and consensus are important ingredients of shared responsibility for ministry. People need to feel some degree of ownership of a project if they are to support it with enthusiasm.

WRITING AN AGENDA

Several thought processes are involved in writing a specific agenda. One relates to planning content, another to allocating time, and a third to organizing content. The whole endeavor is somewhat like developing a family budget. There may be many things we would like to buy or do, but we have limited income. We acknowledge certain expenses as priorities. We subtract the essential or priority items from monthly income in order to determine how much money is left for discretionary purposes. We then have to prioritize our remaining needs according to what we can afford. We eliminate some items as unnecessary and postpone others until we can afford them.

Planning an agenda requires a similar thought process. First, we list all items we might wish to consider; next, we mark those that are priorities. We estimate how much time the priority items will require and subtract that amount of time from the total meeting time available. The amount of time remaining is discretionary. We can then select several items from the list of remaining possibilities. We choose only those that will fit into the time frame of the meeting. Some of the remaining items may need to be eliminated, and others, postponed. We then organize the content appropriately.

PLANNING CONTENT

1. *List all potential items* for inclusion on the agenda.

2. *Prioritize them* based on importance and deadlines.

3. *Identify a single item of highest concern.* There may be several items that you consider to be priorities, but usually one item merits special attention.

4. *Analyze your priority item carefully.* What decisions need to be made? What jobs need to be done? Who will assume responsibility?

ALLOCATING TIME

1. *Estimate time needed for the priority item.* Approximately 30 minutes? 20 minutes?

2. *Add time allocated* for regular activities, such as an opening and closing, with your estimate of time needed for the priority item.

3. *Subtract this sum from the total meeting time available.* This will give you an idea of how much time is left for discussion of lower-priority items.

For example, suppose you usually meet for 1-1/2 hours. Your habit is to use 10 to 15 minutes at the beginning for prayer and sharing and to save 5 minutes at the end for closure. You estimate that 30 minutes will be needed for a priority item. You are therefore allocating approximately 50 minutes for specific items and need to subtract this total from the 90 minutes available.

Opening	15 minutes
Closure	5 minutes
Priority item	+ 30 minutes
Total	50 minutes
Total time available	90 minutes
Time already planned	- 50 minutes
Remainder	40 minutes

Negotiable time remaining—40 minutes—will be allocated next.

4. *Examine remaining topics listed for possible inclusion.* Evaluate each one in the light of its urgency, and estimate time required to discuss it during the meeting.

Suppose you have listed six items that could be included on the agenda in addition to the priority item. One requires reports and decisions; it will probably take 15 minutes. Another requires only a short report; this should only take 5 minutes. Still another relates to long-range planning and requires brainstorming. Creative thinking takes time—at least 20 minutes. The remaining three items would probably require 5 to 10 minutes each.

Since the total estimated time for all six items is approximately 55 to 70 minutes, and since only 40 minutes of the meeting remain in your planning scheme, several of these potential items will have to be postponed.

5. *Select the topics deemed most important for inclusion in the remaining minutes.* Eliminate the other topics and consider them at a later date. Anticipating time requirements and making careful choices enables you to allow sufficient time for priority items and to honor time covenants. If urgent business precludes the possibility of staying within time restraints, notify members in advance that the meeting will likely run longer than usual.

Organizing Content

1. *Sequence agenda items.* Take into consideration peak times of high energy (first half of the meeting) and the need for variety (quick items interspersed with the longer ones to give a sense of progress and movement and to provide change of pace). Then list agenda items in the order you would like to consider them.

2. *Write a first draft.*

3. *Finalize the agenda.* Review your thinking and adjust your plan if necessary.

4. *List the announcements.* These can be written on the agenda and highlighted verbally.

Careful planning is one of the best tools to ensure productive meetings. However, since no leader can perfectly anticipate the flow of a meeting, flexibility is important. The agenda is a guide, but a leader should be prepared to make adjustments when necessary during the meeting. With experience, leaders can learn to plan well, manage time flow, and lead a group to accomplish the work outlined.

The sample agenda on page 146 focuses on a property team's plans to improve the church parking lot. This team project has been under consideration for several months. The purpose of the meeting is to hear reports, review information, and make a decision about bids. The leader uses a simple, clear, three-part format. The priority item appears first, additional items needing consideration are listed next, and finally, announcements are included.

The second sample agenda is for an ad hoc team given the short-term assignment of creating new Christmas decorations for the sanctuary. Team members have already met once. At the first meeting, preliminary brainstorming was done. As ideas were mentioned, members realized that they needed further information in order to take action. They would need to check into cost, possible sources of funding, and even storage space for the new decorations. Members agreed to research the various questions and present information at a follow-up meeting. The agenda on page 147 provides a plan for the follow-up meeting. This plan clearly divides topics into three sections: progress reports (the sharing of information), action items (decision making), and task assignment (the delegation of responsibility).

Agendas will vary depending upon the nature of the work group. A common ingredient of both agendas, however, is a reminder of the congregation's annual goal written at the top. The corporate goal remains important even as groups pursue their own ministry tasks.

PROPERTY TEAM AGENDA

CONGREGATION'S ANNUAL GOAL (brief version):

MEETING DATE:

I. PRIORITY ITEM: Paving the parking lot
   A. Report on bids
   B. Discussion and decision on which bid to accept
   C. Timetable
   D. Alternative parking for members during repair period
   E. Jobs to be done
      1. Write newsletter article regarding timetable for repairs and suggestions for alternative parking during the repair period
      2. Finalize arrangements with contractor
      3. Contact flower shop adjacent to church to request temporary parking privileges during the repair period
      4. Recruit volunteers to paint stripes on the new surface

II. ADDITIONAL ITEMS
   A. Repainting of highway signs
      1. Report: number of signs and estimated cost for painting and repair
      2. Number of volunteers needed
   B. Landscaping on east side of new parking lot
      1. Suggestions and ideas
      2. Volunteers to direct project
   C. Dreams—sharing of ideas related to long-term planning

III. ANNOUNCEMENTS

NOTES:

TIME AND DATE OF NEXT MEETING:

LITURGICAL ARTS TEAM AGENDA

CONGREGATION'S ANNUAL GOAL (brief version):

MEETING DATE:

SHARING AND DEVOTION: Ann Villery

PURPOSE OF MEETING: Finalize plans for sanctuary Christmas decorations

I. REPORTS

  A. Storage space available: Jody

  B. Funds available (gifts and memorials): Peter

  C. Lighting enhancement: Roland

II. DISCUSSION AND DECISIONS

  A. Plan Christmas decorations (in the light of information presented in reports)

  B. Estimate cost of materials and supplies

  C. Discuss ways to recruit workers

  D. Set completion date

III. TASKS ASSIGNED

  A. Purchase materials for new banners

  B. Purchase new garlands and tree decorations

  C. Assemble two teams of helpers to sew and decorate

  D. Supervise sewing

  E. Supervise decorating

  F. Meet with Property Team to arrange placement of new lights

  G. Review plans with the Board of Worship

FUTURE PROJECT: Be thinking of ways we could encourage children to express their faith through art. How might we help them learn the meaning of Christian symbols? Would the Christmas season be a time to initiate such an emphasis, or would we need more time to plan this?

TIME AND DATE OF NEXT MEETING:

AGENDAS FOR GOVERNING BODIES

A governing body must be particularly careful in making wise use of time because of its wide scope of responsibility. Usual items for inclusion are these: minutes, treasurer's report, old business, new business, and committee reports. To maximize available time for business, the president can ask that the minutes and treasurer's report be distributed to members in advance of the meeting. At the meeting itself, the secretary and treasurer can highlight key points verbally. They do not necessarily need to read entire reports.

Again, placing priority items early in the meeting is advisable. Priority business should never be relegated to the last part of the meeting lest it fail to receive the careful consideration it requires. As long as priority items are considered within the first half of the meeting, the actual order of business can be flexible. There is no perfect formula to be set in stone. If the leader incorporates short items among more lengthy ones, the resulting variety will enhance the interest of participants.

One governing body agenda item that commonly absorbs a great amount of time is reports. At best, these reflect the church's ministry and are therefore important ways to keep leaders apprised of activity. At worst, these reports are rambling commentaries by board leaders who have prepared nothing in advance. Many presidents simply "go down the list," asking each chairperson, "Do you have a report for us this evening?" Valuable time is wasted waiting for a reply or listening to an unprepared discourse. Should these reports be eliminated? No! By sharing concerns and activities with the governing body, boards become accountable and solicit support for their projects. Instead of being independent groups doing their own thing, they become part of the whole. Unity of purpose and effort is thereby encouraged. Theoretically then, committee reports should be a valued part of the meeting.

There are several ways to encourage greater responsibility in the area of reporting and thus minimize wasted meeting time. First, the president can request that chairpersons notify him or her a week in advance of the meeting if they wish to have a report included on the agenda. Only those needing to report should then be called upon. Secondly, the governing body can require each board to make a comprehensive report at least once a quarter. The board that is spotlighted can be designated the "board of focus." The advantage of this system is that boards become accountable and cannot hide inactivity in silence. Monthly governing body meetings will thus include one or two comprehensive board reports and then any other reports by those who have requested agenda time.

AGENDA APPROVAL

Acceptance of an agenda by the group is a practice that has gained popularity in recent years. Members are given opportunity for input but not license to ignore the leader's thoughtful preparation. To initiate the business portion of the meeting, the leader gives members an agenda (or provides one in advance). Then, when participants have been given time to glance over the topics to be addressed, the leader asks, "Does anyone wish to amend the agenda?" If no one suggests a change, the group votes to accept the leader's agenda. It is an agreement to adhere to the plan. After the agenda is approved, unrelated topics should not be introduced with the intent of discussing them; generally speaking, once business is underway, new topics should only be suggested for consideration at a future date.

If someone does wish to amend the agenda, the suggestion must be acceptable to the whole group. Suppose, for example, that someone wishes to add an item to the agenda. The suggestion should not be automatically accepted. It is the leader's job to be sure everyone realizes consequences of the proposed change. For example, if the present agenda will fill the time with no spare moments, then adding a major item will require that the group stay beyond the usual time allotted for the meeting. Members must agree that they want to do this if a new item is to be added. Short items may be easily absorbed (with group approval) if the agenda is not overloaded already.

When a change is proposed, the leader presents it to the group and indicates how it will affect the meeting's time schedule. For example, suppose Armand suggests adding discussion on the subject of extending child care an additional thirty minutes on Sunday mornings. The chairperson might reply: "I think we can easily add that subject to our agenda and still maintain the time frame of our meeting. Would the rest of you like to discuss Armand's concern tonight?" Or, perhaps Steve expresses concern about increasing youth participation in worship. The chairperson might reply: "Steve, we can certainly add this to our agenda, but we will probably need to stay longer this evening to do so. Would all of you be able to do that, or shall we put this on the agenda for our next meeting?"

Occasionally an agenda item can be deleted because a member has been unable to procure pertinent information. Leaders should try to contact members with pending reports prior to completing the agenda so that time can be accurately planned, but sometimes unexpected things occur. For example, suppose that when the leader called, Fred thought he could give his report at the meeting but found that unexpected circumstances altered his plans. Fred later says to team members, "I tried my best to gather the data for this report, but I was unable to complete the job. I would like to delay consideration of this matter until the next meeting." The leader then says to the group, "Fred was unable to get all of the information needed. He would like for us to postpone discussion until next month. Would that be all right?" Perhaps the group will say, "Fine," or someone might say, "Well, even if Fred doesn't have all the information ready, I think we need an update because our deadline is coming soon. Perhaps he could share with us whatever he has, even though the report is not complete."

Brief discussion, amendment, and acceptance of the proposed agenda is a valuable way to begin. The initial minutes spent in establishing agreement about items to be considered can bring rich dividends. The leader will be exercising control over the time that follows so that all items will be addressed, but he or she will be doing so with the permission of the participants. They have been given a chance for input and now share in the plan. The agenda becomes a helpful tool, not an imposed structure. Members now have an idea of how much must be accomplished in a given period of time, and they will likely support the leader's efforts to keep discussion moving as the meeting progresses.

A good agenda enables group members to make efficient use of their time together. Preparation of an agenda involves prioritizing concerns, estimating time, eliminating unnecessary items, and making a plan that takes into consideration the need for variety and change of pace.

15

Conducting a Meeting

> A successful meeting preserves an atmosphere of
> mutual respect while engaging members in pur-
> poseful work. The leader's goal is to see that the
> time spent is productive and that participants
> leave with a sense of accomplishment.

As leader, you are the host when members gather to
plan ministry. You are a steward of their time, and as
such, you must see that the hours spent meeting together are worthwhile. Your challenge is to maintain
order, involve all participants in discussion, and guide
the group to decision making and action. You have
work to do, but you also have relationships to nurture;
therefore, you will need to blend understanding with
firmness, social interaction with business, and pleas-
antness with purpose.

Consider the following description of a Music Team meeting called for the purpose of reviewing applications for choir director. Is the meeting time spent productively?

Meeting: Carol, the chairperson, welcomes people as they arrive. Everyone chats amiably about weather, family events, and other news. After fifteen minutes, one of the committee members inquires about applicants for the job. She says, "When you called this meeting, you said we had three responses to our newspaper ad. Can you tell us about them?" Carol smiles, nods affirmatively, and passes out information on three candidates who have applied for the position. Discussion follows. Some talk about their own experiences with choir work in other congregations. One mentions the need for new choir robes. Another talks about the kind of music she prefers as well as the kind she heartily dislikes. Still another speaks of the new choir director at a friend's church. One laments the low salaries generally offered to church musicians. A half-hour passes.

Finally, one of the members asks Carol, "Well, what do *you* think we should do about these applicants? Shall we interview them all?" Carol smiles and shrugs her shoulders. "Whatever you want to do is fine." Again discussion meanders. One member suddenly notices the time and says she needs to leave; others begin to stand up as well and excuse themselves. Noting that a mass exodus is imminent, Carol offers to review résumés herself and make some arrangements. Everyone scurries out the door.

Analysis: What has transpired? There has been animated discussion about many subjects related to church music, but few remarks have been directly pertinent to the topic at hand. Why? In addition, no action has been taken. Why? Answers lie in an evaluation of Carol's leadership. First of all, she did not begin the meeting with a definite gesture, such as a prayer or announcement of the meeting's purpose. Without a clear beginning, members felt free to fill the void with chitchat.

Furthermore, Carol did not interrupt or guide the flow of conversation. She responded to questions but did not assume a leadership role in maintaining focus. She was oblivious to the fact that several of her team members were frustrated that time was being wasted. They wanted to get on with things but didn't want to seem pushy.

> *Replay:* Carol begins the meeting: "Thank you all for coming. Our purpose today is to review applications for the position of choir director and to decide on a course of action. As you know, we have had three applicants. Our hope is to secure a new director by the end of July. That gives us only four more weeks to conduct our search, so today we will want to work out a plan. First of all, let's review these applications together. Then let's decide if we want to interview all of the candidates or only some of them. Finally, we'll set up our dates for interviews and decide how to proceed." The group then discusses each application and makes plans that are pertinent and focused.

In the first account, Carol abdicated her leadership responsibility. She did not clearly define the purpose of the meeting nor guide members in meaningful activity. The meeting concluded with no action having been taken. In the replay version, Carol initiated a purposeful meeting focused on problem solving. She began by announcing the purpose at the meeting and by explaining the procedure to be followed. Members left feeling they had made significant progress. They accomplished an important task in the time they spent together.

PREPARING FOR THE MEETING

As a leader, your own preparation begins long before the meeting date. Preparing includes anticipating needs and problems, contacting people, making arrangements, and planning details. The following checklist of tasks can serve as a guide:

1. Remind members of the upcoming meeting with postcards or phone calls. Even when groups have a regular meeting time, reminders help ensure attendance. This is a job that can be delegated.

2. Alert those members who will need to give reports or lead devotions.

3. Prepare an agenda.

4. Arrive early to see that the room temperature is comfortable and that chairs are arranged in a desirable manner.

5. Write the agenda on a chalkboard if you do not have it on paper for each person.

BEGINNING THE MEETING

• *Start on time.* Promptness in starting the meeting shows respect for people's time. A meeting should always begin at the designated hour. Waiting for stragglers conditions them to continue to arrive late. If your meeting is set for 7:00 P.M. and someone arrives at 7:15 several months in a row, ask him privately if 7:00 is too early. "Rob, I notice that 7:00 seems to be a bit early for your schedule. Would it help you if we met at 7:15 or 7:30 instead?" This will indicate to the member that you desire punctuality and that you view the opening moments as important.

• *Provide a transition time.* A period of ten minutes for sharing at the beginning of the meeting can contribute greatly to group unity. It can be a time for building bonds of trust and understanding. If, however, this effort is not meaningful but becomes a time for random chitchat, some members of the committee will quickly decide that the first ten minutes is wasted time, and they will come ten minutes late when, in their opinion, the meeting really starts. At the outset, explain to committee members your intention to use the first ten minutes for sharing so that members can get to know each other better in the process of working together.

People coming together from different experiences usually need time to shift their thoughts from daily activity to the concerns of the meeting. One may have had to skip a meal to arrive on time. Another may have a sick child. Still another may be distracted by marital problems. Another may be jubilant over news of a scholarship for her daughter. And so it goes. Transition time provides a chance to settle down, to get in touch with each other, to help individuals feel valued for more than their contribution of time to the work of the church.

Plan your approach. "How are you tonight?" will probably elicit a one word answer: "Fine." Instead, you could ask, "Does anyone have any good news to share?" People might mention a promotion at work, a child's improvement in school, a birthday or anniversary, a spiritual insight or experience, and so on. You can also ask, "Are there any special concerns?" Job stress, family problems, and illness are all things that may be mentioned. As members begin to see each other as persons with problems and joys similar to their own, they will learn to care for one another. This concept is somewhat rare in today's society; we often spin from one event to another, focusing on tasks and neglecting relationships.

This time of sharing should not feel contrived or awkward. It should be gentle, voluntary, and not forced. If someone doesn't wish to say anything, accept that. Often it helps if the leader sets the tone by sharing first. This sharing will become spontaneous in time. It should not feel mechanical, with the leader asking the same questions every time. Variation and creative approaches encourage responsiveness.

Personal problems should not significantly alter the course of a business meeting except on rare occasions. Occasionally a personal crisis may warrant an interruption of the meeting; people need to stop and minister to the troubled person. Usually, however, you can give the situation appropriate attention and then resume the work of the meeting; lingering afterwards to express concern is better than abandoning the agenda completely and rescheduling the meeting. Your primary responsibility is to respect the time investment of the whole group by moving the meeting along. Unless circumstances are extremely unusual, you would be unwise to forsake this goal.

• *Plan a spiritual focus.* After the sharing time, begin the meeting with a prayer or short devotion. This task can be assigned to one particular person or rotated among members; you can also use a sentence prayer with all members participating. We often take agreement of purpose for granted: "We all know why we are here." Experience indicates that the opposite is often true. Not only do we forget why we gather, but we easily get sidetracked once we begin. We need to be reminded of mission and purpose. A prayer or a devotion will collect group thoughts and focus them on God's work.

Conducting Business

• *Ask the group to accept the agenda.* This is a practice that allows members to alter and/or approve plans for the meeting. Once agreement is reached, members adhere to the agenda and thus give you permission to exercise control over time and topics. This procedure usually takes only a few minutes.

• *Remind people of the meeting's main purpose.* Although many items may be on the agenda, you should verbally underscore the one(s) that will be emphasized.

• *Be enthusiastic as you speak.* Your mood sets the tone for the meeting. Enthusiasm is a wonderful magnet that draws positive response from others. It is true that leaders, like anyone else, suffer from fatigue and discouragement at times. If at all possible, however, a leader should try to put aside these feelings when conducting a meeting. A leader who smiles and seems excited will infect the whole group with a "can do" spirit; conversely, one who is tired, grumpy, or negative will cause the group to feel downhearted and lethargic. Stir up the coals and the fire will ignite!

• *Communicate clearly.* Whether a meeting is informal or formal in structure, verbal skill facilitates action. If ideas are presented well, they are more apt to meet with approval. As leader, you can avoid some of the confusion or hurt feelings that result when people do not understand proposals. Explain ideas as clearly as possible and repeat the information if necessary. Sometimes we assume that others know things when, in fact, they do not. It is better to explain something people may already know than to risk confusion and delay.

• *Ask questions that are specific and clear.* Sometimes leaders cause confusion by asking vague questions. For example, "What do you want to do about the Sunday School Christmas program this year?" Does this mean, "Do you want to have one this year?" or "What type of program shall we have this year?" or "When shall we have it?" or "Who could direct it this year?" If listeners must puzzle over meaning, time will be wasted with clarification before they can respond.

• *Use visual reinforcement when possible.* Write important dates or details on the agenda itself or on a chalkboard. Some people have difficulty retaining verbal information, but if they see it written, they are more likely to remember. Encourage notetaking by furnishing pencils and by leaving ample space on the agenda for additions.

GUIDING DISCUSSION

Discussion is a major component of most meetings and is vital to group work; it stirs up creativity and makes use of the variety of experiences, talents, and perspectives of members.

Synergy is a term used to describe the idea that the sum of the parts is greater than any individual part. In other words, a person may be capable of tackling a job without help, but if that person works with others, the sum of their corporate endeavor may well surpass any result he or she could produce alone. Hence, ideas generated by a group are likely to produce better results than ideas generated by an individual.

A leader's challenge, therefore, is to provide an atmosphere in which everyone can contribute ideas and to guide discussion so that it is focused and productive. Unless a leader guides the group toward decision making or at least summarizes points made during discussion, the ideas expressed may be forgotten.

TIPS FOR LEADING GROUP DISCUSSION

1. Listen. Be attentive when others speak; indicate interest by making good eye contact and by responding to comments.

2. Appreciate input. With appropriate words and gestures, such as a smile or a nod, affirm those who contribute.

3. Prevent domination. If someone monopolizes discussion, the leader needs to intervene. A kind but firm response will terminate the commentary and allow the group to move on. For instance, "Thank you. What you say is an important consideration. What do the rest of you think?" or "Could we sum up your thoughts by saying . . . ? Now, would others of you like to share your thoughts about this issue?"

4. Clarify. Sometimes a person shares thoughts that are not clear. When that happens, others may indicate by facial expressions that they have not understood. At that point the leader can rephrase the comment or ask for clarification. "Are you saying that . . . ?"

5. Redirect questions. Sometimes individuals ask the leader questions that should be redirected to the whole group. For instance, suppose a member firmly addresses the leader with these words: "I don't think we should use the same type of stewardship drive we used last year, do you?" His own negative opinion is evident in both his words and the tone of his voice; he obviously hopes to elicit support for his position from the leader. If the leader agrees or disagrees in an initial response, the rest of the members may feel intimidated. Instead of answering immediately with a clear "yes" or "no," the leader may redirect the question to the whole group. "What do the rest of you think?" or "How do the rest of you feel about repeating last year's program?"

In other words, not all questions directed to the leader need to be answered by the leader. If the questions seek factual information, the leader may need to answer, but if the questions seek an opinion, perhaps they should be considered by all participants. The leader's opinion may indeed be shared with the group, but not always as the first response lest it preclude further input. The leader can redirect the question, allow for other comments, and then add his or her own opinion in conclusion.

6. Make connections between points made by different people. By showing how comments relate to one another, we promote understanding. People do not always see how their ideas correlate with those expressed by other people. "I think what you are saying, Peter, expresses the same concern that Gary voiced a few minutes ago . . . that a change in our worship schedule at this time would be premature." Or, "Mike, your concern for timing relates to Joanne's earlier comments about the congregation that neglected its youth ministry and subsequently lost many young families."

7. Summarize. Put into a brief statement a summary of collective thought so that members have an opportunity to see if people are perceiving conversation in the same way. "It seems to me that we are in agreement then. We all believe that we should go ahead with the building plan presented last night." Or, "Would it be accurate, then, to say that we want to expand our summer Vacation Bible School program to two weeks as well as include seventh and eighth graders?" This brings closure to the discussion and allows for final reservations or dissent to be voiced.

8. Watch the time. A leader needs to intervene when sufficient discussion has taken place and ask the group whether or not they are ready to make a decision on the matter at hand. One might say, "I think we have heard a wide variety of opinions on this matter. Are you ready to make a decision?" Or, "Since we have had a lengthy discussion and other items remain on our agenda, are you ready to take action on this issue?"

9. Recognize and counter blocking behaviors. There are many behaviors that can hinder and destroy a group's ability to work together effectively. Some can be dealt with by the leader or by group members during the meeting. Others may require a private conversation between the leader and the offending persons. Blocking behaviors cause a group to become uncomfortable and unfocused. If someone is perpetually negative, opinionated, hostile, intolerant, or petty, the group's ability to proceed is hampered. Other blocking behaviors include digressing, interrupting, monopolizing, and clowning. Each of these disrupts and leads to frustration within the group. A leader needs to intervene when these behaviors occur.

10. *Be sensitive to nonverbal communication.* Recognize and respond to signals that are clues to people's thoughts. What signals do you give with your own facial expressions and body language when you disagree or are feeling bored, tired, or angry? Others use the same signals. Leaders who are aware of changes in the demeanor of group members while a meeting is in progress can respond appropriately.

You should never become so preoccupied with conducting the meeting that the reactions of others are overlooked. Awareness of subtle physical clues helps you deal sensitively with group members. For example, sometimes you can read the face of someone who wants to speak but cannot find opportunity. You can then address the person as soon as possible. If someone appears to be in disagreement but does not choose to voice his or her thoughts to the group, you can follow up if the situation seems to warrant further attention. Follow-up can be done in private conversation after the meeting or possibly in a phone call the next day.

Closure

Closure should be definite and clear. A meeting that simply dwindles away leaves members unsure about what has been accomplished. Ideas may be forgotten and bear no fruit. Any of the following may be used to bring closure to a meeting.

- *Summary of key decisions:* Review action taken.

- *Reminders:* Mention important dates or deadlines.

- *Review of work assignments:* Mention names of those who are assuming responsibility for tasks; be sure they have a completion date in mind.

- *Appreciation:* Thank members for being there and for the work they accomplished. By giving credit in the context of the meeting, you underscore the value of their work and encourage them to continue.

• *Prayer:* Lead members in a brief closing prayer.

FOLLOW-UP

Respond promptly to group decisions in order to maintain group momentum and spirit. If you procrastinate, members of the board or team may lose heart. Many times the enthusiasm of good ideas evaporates when those responsible for setting the plans in motion postpone their responsibilities.

Leaders conduct meetings effectively when they plan with care, communicate clearly, guide discussion so that all can participate, and move the group toward decision making.

16

Conflict Resolution

Conflict in the church is inevitable. Differences in values, beliefs, opinions, and desires exist wherever humans gather. Conflict resolution attempts to recognize those differences, manage them, and prevent them from becoming divisive.

Although conflict is frequently perceived as being negative and harmful, Scripture and our own lives bear witness to the fact that God's people often experience dramatic moments of redemption and revelation in the context of conflict. In organizational work, conflict can be a helpful factor in decision making because it prompts us to examine opposing ideas and alternatives before making a judgment. It can provide a creative tension that broadens our thinking and is a catalyst for growth.

Conflict becomes destructive only when people fail to seek common ground and understanding. When one or more persons in a group become alienated because of their differences, the whole group suffers. Conflict can easily escalate and cause damage that lasts for years. Because unresolved conflict carries a potential for significant damage to both individuals and groups, it cannot be ignored. Leaders have an important role to play in halting its potentially destructive course.

Conflict is never generic in nature. Each situation has specific and unique characteristics. People disagree with one another because they have different beliefs, experiences, needs, and desires that cause them to develop their own goals and priorities. A leader who identifies the underlying causes of a particular conflict can mediate more effectively.

ROOTS OF CONFLICT—OUR DIFFERENCES

• *Beliefs*—A common cause of conflict is disagreement over beliefs. Beliefs are usually conclusions people have reached over a long period of time, and they often can be traced back to childhood teaching or family tradition. Conflict arising from opposing beliefs is sometimes difficult to resolve. The mediator's tool is skill in communicating—skill in helping each side express thoughts clearly. The goal is not necessarily to reach agreement, but rather to help the conflicted parties understand and consider one another's viewpoints.

• *Experiences*—People sometimes approach decisions with prejudice; they are unable to be objective in the present because of past experiences. They believe that what failed before will probably fail again. They also may attempt to transfer successes of past situations to the present without realizing that what worked in one place does not necessarily work in another. When prejudgment results in conflict, resolution requires helping those involved to look objectively at all aspects of the matter under consideration so that a reasonable conclusion can be drawn. Adequate information is important in helping both sides understand the issues clearly and consider alternative proposals.

• *Needs*—Differing needs can also generate conflict. At various stages of life people view certain activities as more important than others. Whereas more adequate furniture for the nursery might be a top priority for parents of young children, a new sound system in the sanctuary might be more important to some of the older members. When needs clash and resources are limited, conflict resolution involves evaluating the situation to determine which need is more urgent. An effective leader affirms as valid the various needs mentioned and expresses regret that resources do not permit addressing all of these needs at once. The goal of mediation will be to help members develop a plan for the future that takes into account diverse needs and that establishes clear priorities.

• *Desires*—Personal preferences can also clash, creating conflict. People want certain things done a particular way simply because it suits them better. They may become quite vocal regarding such things as music, times of worship, or communion practices because they have strong personal preferences. When the desires of one person clash with those of someone else, conflict resolution requires compromise. Often this involves mediating while both sides explain reasons for their positions. Hopefully, increased understanding will lead to an acceptable solution. A leader sometimes needs to remind opponents that give and take is a part of life.

CONFLICT'S POTENTIAL FOR DAMAGE

Conflict can incite us to behave in ways that separate us from one another. We may begin to dislike others simply because we disagree with their ideas. The more emotional we become, the less likely we are to communicate effectively. Eventually, a situation may become "us versus them," a personal confrontation rather than an effort to resolve an issue. One clue that a potentially damaging situation is developing is that one or more of the parties involved is overreacting with vehemence that exceeds the issue's merits.

When different perspectives are driven by personalized anger, the conflict becomes destructive. Issues are unlikely to be settled unless the anger is addressed, and until damaged relationships are repaired, new issues will keep appearing and dividing the conflicted parties.

At church, a conflict's potential for damage increases when those involved use gossip or negative talk to pressure others into taking sides. The result of widespread agitation and discontent is usually a no-win situation. Once a significant division develops, resolution may not be possible. Whole churches have fallen prey to divisiveness when people have taken sides on issues that have become emotionally charged. It is important for leaders to identify and deal with significant problems in their formative stages rather than to avoid problems with the hope that they'll simply go away.

GRIEVANCES AND OPPOSITION

• *Complaints and misunderstandings*—Major problems often ignite from a single complaint or incident. As leaders, we probably will be called upon now and then to listen and respond to hurts or misunderstandings. Our willingness simply to hear a person's grievance is sometimes sufficient help. But the way we listen is important! There are always two sides to disputes, two perceptions of truth. We are not usually in a position to give advice or opinions when we have heard only one version of an incident. Therefore, we should withhold judgment in the initial stages.

When a member comes to us with complaints, we should listen carefully. We should express concern and understanding, but we should not reinforce the person's negative feelings or make hasty judgments. Sometimes we can provide information that sheds new light on the problem. We also can ask questions to help the offended person clarify his or her perceptions. When discussion reaches the problem-solving stage, we can work with the person to find a solution. We do not have to provide answers, but we may certainly offer suggestions if asked. It is usually best to let the offended person figure out a course of action since he or she must live with the solution.

A follow-up conversation is advisable. After several days have passed, a wise leader checks with the person who was upset to see what progress has been made. Continuing concern and interest by a leader helps alleviate the offended person's distress.

If a problem seems urgent or persists, we can encourage the one who is upset to talk directly with the offending members; we may even offer to go along. Clear guidelines for resolving serious conflict are given to us in Matthew 18:15–20. Jesus admonishes us to work out grievances directly and quickly. Dealing with the problem forthrightly is far better than spreading ill will by gossiping or complaining to others.

• *Open hostility*—Intervention is certainly warranted when differences erupt into angry confrontation within a group. Heated argument should not be allowed to continue during a meeting. As leaders, we should interrupt the argument and ask the parties involved to postpone the discussion. In terminating the argument, we should not demean those involved. Instead, we can underscore the desire of the group to hear both sides but suggest that tabling the discussion would give all concerned a chance to give further consideration to the issue.

Prompt follow-up by the leader may be necessary to initiate the process of reconciliation. If negative feelings fester, they may become so ingrained that those involved cannot be coaxed to move back into harmony. Therefore, soon after the episode occurs, we should contact those involved and arrange to meet with them apart from the committee context. One advantage of this separate meeting is that those who are in conflict will understand that we care about them and about their viewpoints. They will also be more likely to communicate well in a less threatening setting with no bystanders. Mediation involves protecting the right of each to speak without interruption. Our task is to help each person understand the other's point of view so that anger is diffused before the next committee meeting. If no action is taken to resolve the problem, the group's work will continue to be blocked by animosity.

• *Subtle opposition*—Sometimes people express anger or discontent without being openly hostile. Indirect opposition may be less noticeable than direct confrontation, but it can be equally destructive to a group. Criticizing group members behind their backs, circulating rumors, or intentionally blocking progress are all tactics that undermine a group's ability to work.

We often ignore such subtle opposition and consider it simply an aggravation. We minimize its importance, postpone intervention, and hope the problem will simply go away. We all dread unpleasantness, but the truth is that once we recognize the existence of antagonistic behavior, we need to address it as surely as we address open hostility. Subtle erosion of spirit can be just as harmful to a group as open conflict in meetings. The journey to disaster may be slower, but the results will be equally devastating.

It is important to have an open mind when addressing problems related to conflict. Otherwise, we may misconstrue circumstances and motivation and be tempted to reach conclusions prematurely. As leaders, we must remain impartial as we listen to explanations. The purpose of intervention is to encourage and support reconciliation. The healing and vitality of relationships takes priority in the Body of Christ. This means that we do not seek to punish or condemn but rather to restore harmonious and understanding relationships.

A LEADER'S ROLE IN CONFLICT RESOLUTION

As leaders, our role in conflict situations can be that of mediator. As such, we gather information by listening carefully and encourage both sides to create a fair settlement. The goal is to bring differences under close scrutiny and to seek understanding and resolution. Therefore, power is not an appropriate tool. If we enter the fray simply with authority of position, not only may those involved feel intimidated or further frustrated, but we also risk getting caught in the middle. We might forge a temporary truce, but lasting peace will come only when those with divergent views have ample chance to dialogue, question, compromise, and forgive what needs forgiveness. Conflict is not resolved if it is merely suppressed to buy peace.

Therefore, our task in resolving conflict is to create a supportive environment in which both sides can talk and seek compromise. We clarify what is said and help to find solutions. Perhaps the views of one side will not be fully accepted by the other side, but if they are understood and valued, progress can be made. Success occurs when mutual understanding is achieved and when both sides can continue working together.

The leader's challenge is to guide exploration of differences in a calm manner so that healing can occur. An ability to maintain self-control, to avoid siding with participants, and to show respect for the people involved is key to being effective in conflict situations. The conflict is important to those involved and must be treated as such by a mediator. Patience is another asset in mediating since the process often requires several meetings. The goal is to help both sides get to the core of their disrupted relationship and move toward harmony.

CONFLICT RESOLUTION SKILLS

Leaders need both verbal skills and wisdom when working to resolve conflict. Each aspect of the process requires sensitivity, tact, discernment, and patience. Below is a list of essential communication and problem-solving skills.

1. Ability to initiate confrontation—A leader needs to be able to effectively express concern and pose questions that open a subject for discussion. Consider the following possibilities for initiating dialogue:

> John, lately you've seemed withdrawn in our meetings. Has something or someone offended you? If so, can we talk it over?

OR

> Tracy, is it true that you're considering resigning from your teaching position because some of the children continue to misbehave? You're an important member of our staff, and I'd like to help you if I can. Could we talk about some possible solutions to the problem?

2. Ability to listen and clarify—People who are angry often want someone to understand their point of view. A leader needs to listen actively and to restate their position to let them know that the comments have been clearly understood. Further clarification may be warranted if they persist in misinterpreting the situation or others' motives.

> George, I can understand your desire to resign from the Building Committee. You say no one listens to your views, and you've grown tired of working with the

group because they don't seem interested in your ideas about cutting costs. Is that the main reason—that they don't seem to respect your ideas?

3. *Ability to diagnose the nature of the conflict*—Are the participants really arguing about a particular issue, or are there underlying problems creating or adding to the tension? Sometimes the real problem is an earlier affront or unspoken grievance. The leader may need to ask, "Why is this bothering you so much? Is there some other reason for your frustration?"

4. *Ability to negotiate*—Once the problem has been clarified, what are some possible solutions? What are the real needs and limits of either side? Is compromise possible? If both sides in the disagreement take ownership of the problem-solving phase, there is a better chance of reconciliation and harmony.

> Linda and Doug, you both oppose starting a day-care center. You have mentioned some important disadvantages and concerns. However, Ken and Peggy hold equally strong opinions about the merit of such a program. Could we study the issue more carefully? Perhaps we could visit churches in our area that have started day-care centers. We could discover what their experience has been, both positive and negative. How would you feel about our doing that together before we make a final decision?

CONFLICT AND DECISION MAKING

Some issues in congregational life stir up controversy and produce a strong emotional response in members. Forcing a vote in the context of major conflict may have dire consequences. For example, suppose one congregation is struggling over the issue of relocating the church. Major debate paralyzes members. Some want to preserve the present facility; others see greater opportunity for growth in a new location. Leaders also hold divergent viewpoints and are unable to agree on a proposal to present to the congregation. Making a decision under these conditions risks alienating a segment of the congregation. What alternatives are there?

One option is to postpone voting. Time and communication are the tools of amelioration when dissension threatens stability. Postponement of decision making allows time for further thought and for calming of emotions. Issues which are sensitive in nature may require a longer period of reflection. If at all possible, postpone action when there is much uneasiness or dissension present, but use the interim productively! Delay should bring specific benefits. Leaders can gather additional information, bring in guests who can shed light on the issue, visit other facilities that may have the features you are considering, or simply provide forums for open discussion and debate so that views can be further clarified. In other words, opposition or uncertainty is more likely to change during a postponement period if there is further discussion and new input.

Another option is to gear voting procedures to accommodate difficult situations. Majority rule and consensus are different ways to make group decisions. Each has both advantages and disadvantages that should be taken into consideration in the midst of conflict.

Majority rule means that action can be taken if at least one more person votes for a proposal than votes against it. For the sake of expediency, we use majority rule to make routine decisions at all levels—in committees, on council, and in congregational meetings. The obvious advantage is that decisions can be made quickly, as soon as at least one person can break a tie. The disadvantage, however, is that forcing a decision when a large number of people vehemently disagree will probably result in ongoing conflict, especially when the issue involved will impact a great many people. Residual feelings of discontent may cause those who oppose the action to gripe and complain. A plan that was approved by a narrow margin may fail during the implementation stage from lack of support.

Majority rule is best used in routine decision making by small groups and in large groups when an issue has not produced major conflict. If significant conflict exists in a large group, the only alternative is to postpone action until further information can be gathered and discussion held. Smaller groups have another option: consensus.

Consensus means that those voting are in complete agreement. Persuasion, reasoning, and compromise eventually convince sides to join in a unified position. This method can be useful within the governing body when important decisions must be made. When leaders are unified in support of a proposal, that proposal has added strength when presented to members at large. Consensus can be a more time-consuming way to make decisions. Action is often delayed and even may not be possible in certain circumstances. There is an important advantage, however. If there is widespread support for the project at its inception, there will probably be continued support during implementation. Once convinced that a particular course of action is wise, leaders can then present their proposals to the congregation with enthusiasm and confidence.

When should consensus be used? Consensus is usually not possible at the congregational level; however, it can be useful in governing bodies and occasionally in committees. Some governing bodies use consensus for all major decisions even though action may be postponed in the attempt to reach agreement. For them, preserving unity is a higher goal than prompt action. If the following conditions exist, leaders should consider waiting for consensus: the decision relates to a sensitive issue which will affect everyone; sharp division of opinion or confusion exists; considerable financial outlay is involved. Under such circumstances, leaders should consider using consensus unless constitutional requirements mandate a particular voting procedure.

Suppose leaders are considering a proposal to add a second worship service. Some members cite strong reasons why such a change would be beneficial, but others voice equally strong reasons why such a change might be detrimental. People become emotional and upset during the discussion preceding the vote. Would it be wise to make a decision using majority rule? It would be best to delay the vote until consensus could be achieved or until a later date when majority rule would be less divisive. If leaders are uncertain about a particular course of action, they cannot present it effectively to the body at large.

The way decisions are made on all levels of church organization certainly has a direct bearing on attitudes and response. If we allow sufficient time for discussion, gather information, and adapt voting procedures to the situation, we will minimize the chance of alienating members or producing divisiveness in the congregation. Every attempt should be made to handle things fairly and without pressure as people work through the process of decision making.

Conflict exists at some time or another in all group situations. A leader's challenge is to use differences for growth and problem solving and to handle voting in a judicious manner.

17

DELEGATING AND
ACCOUNTABILITY

Sharing the workload allows us to share the joy of
ministry. We involve others so they can learn,
serve, and witness. Holding ourselves and others
accountable encourages us to be good stewards of
the area of ministry entrusted to us.

Isn't delegating rather risky? Although the idea of sharing our work with others may sound appealing, we
sometimes have reservations based on previous experiences. All of us have known disappointment when we
have depended on a co-worker and then found that he
or she has forgotten, neglected, or decided not to do the
task. If this happens several times, we may be tempted
to say, "I'd rather just do it myself!" When we share
responsibility with others, we do run the risk of being
disappointed; however, the benefits of sharing our ministry outweighs the risks.

BENEFITS OF DELEGATING

Delegating involves distributing work and entrusting others with responsibility. The benefits are significant! First of all, sharing the workload helps leaders conserve their own energy. Burnout is a common result of working alone. Many of us know of instances when people have dropped out of a congregation after a demanding period of leadership. These persons may have felt overworked and unappreciated because they lacked sufficient help. Perhaps failure to delegate contributed to their fatigue. Although many factors can contribute to discouragement and strain, delegating effectively is one way to guard against these problems. If work can be divided into small areas of responsibility, many people can contribute time and energy and thus minimize the leader's fatigue.

Delegating also helps us develop a broader base of support for our work. People who give time to a project usually take a personal interest in its success and are more likely to promote it with enthusiasm.

Another benefit of delegating is that when we involve others, we tap into a wider reservoir of ideas, talents, and experiences. We multiply creative possibilities. Others may be able to provide skills that we do not have and thus contribute exciting, new dimensions to the project.

Finally, delegating has a long-term benefit for the congregation. It is an investment in leadership development. When we delegate responsibility for a task, we generally continue working with those people, providing them with information and counsel. Inexperienced members are much more likely to help if they know an interested leader will be there to lend support. This on-the-job training provides people with knowledge, skills, and experience that can enable them to assume leadership roles in the future.

Risk Factors

Is delegating risky? Certainly! Some of us may be convinced of the validity of delegation but have reservations based on our own need to succeed or on past attempts that failed.

Perhaps we hesitate because we have high standards and like things done a particular way. We know that whatever moves out of our control and into the hands of another cannot be guaranteed. Someone else may not do a job the way we had hoped. Someone else may not be dependable. We are hesitant, therefore, to relinquish any part of our responsibility and risk an uncertain outcome.

More often we are reluctant to delegate because we don't know how to do it. Perhaps we have tried and failed and are therefore afraid to try again. We may have thought that delegating was simply assigning tasks. Suppose, for example, that you are in charge of a congregational fund-raising dinner. You can divide areas of responsibility into several categories: invitations, publicity, decorations, food preparation, setup and cleanup, and program. If you ask others to assume responsibility for each task, isn't that delegating? Not really . . . at least, it is not delegating that is likely to work. Delegating that is effective involves much more than merely dividing the workload.

The Solution: Partnership

Delegating is a continuing partnership between the leader and those who have assumed responsibility. For example, if you ask Mary to send out invitations for the dinner, you still bear ultimate responsibility for the task since you are in charge of the project; therefore, you need to help Mary with initial planning and check with her periodically to be sure her work is being done. This doesn't mean hovering or harassing, but it does mean that you speak with her periodically to see how she's doing and to encourage her.

Delegating always requires progress checks. If a person is asked to do a job but is shown minimal interest and support thereafter, the person may well assume that no one cares! Therefore, why bother? A leader who delegates must continue to show interest and support to everyone who is assuming responsibility.

Effective delegating involves communication during planning, supervision during implementation, and follow-up when work has been completed. Leaders should be available at all times to answer questions, give advice, and oversee work.

Specific aspects of delegating include

- assigning tasks to others
- requiring accountability
- supervising
- encouraging
- commending

A leader needs to be aware of each of these important ingredients. Overlooking any of them can bring disappointing results. The amount of input needed will depend on the experience and ability of the person who assumes responsibility for the task. But even if that person is extremely capable, a leader needs to be informed about decisions and aware of plans.

TIPS FOR EFFECTIVE DELEGATION

1. Find the right person to do the job. Paramount is the need to find persons who are capable of doing a good job and who truly want to contribute their efforts. When you ask someone to take on a responsibility, therefore, look for interest and desire, not just willingness, and be willing to accept someone's choice not to participate.

2. Explain the task well. Anyone who is asked to take a job needs to know what level of effort it will require and why the job is important. Provide a clear description of the task, preferably in writing. People do not always retain verbal information easily. They appreciate having something written down as a reference.

3. Seek a response without applying pressure. If you pressure reluctant people into service, do not be surprised if they fail to do work on time or well. Certainly, to enlist help, you should have some convincing reasons for why a person should consider volunteering his or her time, but convincing others to help is not the ultimate goal.

4. Foresee obstacles and/or constraints. Once someone accepts a delegated task, explain any special limitations. It is extremely important that constraints be clearly understood, particularly if wide latitude is being given on how objectives are to be accomplished. Mention factors such as money, space, time, policy, rules, or traditions which might be relevant to the task. Careful instruction will prevent embarrassment that can result when a plan is rejected because it contradicts policy. For example, if no money is available for a project, then the chairperson needs to know that donations will be necessary. If a youth activity is being planned, the chairperson needs to know that your church has a policy that prohibits dancing in the fellowship hall. If the congregation has certain rituals connected with Christmas Eve service, then the new worship chairperson needs to know of those traditions when planning.

5. Offer advice and counsel along the way if workers ask for input. If Carlos asks a question about publicity, don't reply, "Oh, do whatever you want. I'm sure it will be fine." Carlos is asking because he wants advice.

6. Be sure deadlines are clear. Leave nothing to chance. If the task you are delegating requires meeting multiple deadlines, you should work out a timetable with the person. For instance, suppose you ask someone to serve as director of Vacation Bible School. This job requires attention to deadlines and skill with time management. Materials must be ordered, teachers recruited, dates publicized, registration planned, craft supplies purchased, and staff training sessions held. As leader, you may need to review deadlines with the director and touch base periodically to see whether things are moving along as planned.

7. *Evaluate a project once it is completed.* Review the project with those to whom the work was delegated. What problems were encountered? How many people attended? How could the planning and development sequence be improved? What was especially successful? What would you do differently next time, and what additional resources might be useful? An organized report provides an invaluable tool for planning similar events in the future.

8. *Appreciate the effort made.* Appropriate and intentional recognition is important because it encourages volunteers.

Coordinating Team Activity

Deadlines usually have to be met to ensure team success. If one job is not done, the next may be undermined; there is a domino effect that hinders everyone involved in a project. It is therefore imperative that team activities be coordinated. Calendars and timetables are visual tools that encourage effective use of time. They assist project planners in assessing the time available for completion of a project. Because they can be used to show a work sequence from a project's inception to its completion, they can also help leaders track progress. It is wise, therefore, to utilize them both in the initial stages of planning and as work on a project progresses. Suppose, for example, that a committee meets to plan a celebration of the church's twenty-fifth anniversary. If the team begins planning in October and the anniversary celebration is to be held in June, then a nine-month period is available. The team lists all tasks related to the celebration and then creates a step-by-step progression by asking, "What needs to be done by year's end? In January? In February?" and so on. As each successive month is planned, those involved are able to see when their own particular deadlines occur. After plans are finalized and work begins, workers will be able to look at the calendar or timetable when they gather and see if all is on schedule.

ACCOUNTABILITY

Biblically, the basis for accountability is that one day all people will be accountable before God for their lives. To be accountable is to be answerable—to give reason for what we have done or left undone. Whether we are responsible for an entire area of church life or for a small event in the course of a year, we are stewards of God's resources and are responsible for doing our work well.

SETTING AN EXAMPLE

Members of a team generally take their cues from the leader's work habits. They pick up attitudes and behaviors while working with the chairperson. We cannot effectively hold others accountable if we ourselves are lackadaisical in our leadership work. Our own dependability, involvement, and record keeping provide stability and backbone for organizational work. We demonstrate our accountability in a number of specific ways:

• *By being reliable*—Our committee members need to know that we can be counted upon to do what we have said we will do. They will appreciate the blessing that dependability brings to organizational work. Our example should motivate them to be reliable as well.

• *By being prompt*— If we are slow in doing our part of a task, others will probably become lackadaisical as well and possibly delay the project's completion. Our own attention to deadlines shows a commitment to the plan and to others working on the project.

• *By communicating well*—Our goal as leaders is to help committee members operate as a team rather than as satellites spinning in independent orbits. Therefore, if we make every effort to convey helpful information and provide frequent progress updates, team members will be spared unnecessary anxiety, and duplication of effort will be minimized.

• *By keeping records up-to-date*—Well-kept records show that we are interested, informed, and concerned about the task. Reports of money spent, helpers needed, supplies purchased, and action steps taken can provide both a record of progress and a valuable tool for future reference. Not only should we maintain a paper trail as work progresses, but we should also prepare a summary report when the work is completed.

HOLDING OTHERS ACCOUNTABLE

Delegating is sharing the stewardship of a project. It requires accountability because ministry is too important to leave to chance. If someone fails to do a task, other people will likely be affected. In the church we often go to great lengths to avoid hurting others' feelings. Therefore, if someone accepts a responsibility but does nothing at all, we are reluctant to confront the person. To ensure successful ministry, however, we must learn to supervise progress and see that others carry out their responsibilities faithfully. People on all levels of organizational life need to know that there are expectations and that they will be held accountable for their work.

We are less likely to neglect a task or minimize its importance if we know in advance that we will need to review our work with others. When a leader requires input and reports, team members are more likely to share the workload equitably. When a leader does not seem to care about the degree to which people commit themselves, some persons will be lazy while others work harder. As leaders, we should not ask people to do more than they are able, but we certainly should let them know that we expect them to do whatever they can. Different levels of participation certainly are acceptable, but co-workers need to know that we expect them to follow through on their responsibilities.

Supervision gives an aura of importance to job assignments. People are less likely to neglect something that is deemed important by others and for which they will be accountable at a specific time.

HANDLING NEGLIGENCE

Members may disappoint us by neglecting their responsibilities. They have excuses. Sometimes they fail to attend meetings and simply drop out. This usually happens when people accept jobs they really do not want. Sometimes they accept with good intentions but later find they are overcommitted and do not know how to extricate themselves from unwanted responsibility. There is no way to overemphasize the importance of seeking at the outset workers who are interested in serving. If, however, someone abdicates responsibility once he or she has agreed to serve, a leader needs to remedy the problem.

Approaching such a person is a delicate matter. The first priority should be concern for the person. Find out what the problem seems to be. Before jumping to conclusions, give him or her an opportunity to explain in the event that there are personal reasons for apathy. A second priority should be concern for the project. Ask if the person has questions about the job or would like additional help. Many times people fail to carry out responsibility because they do not know what to do and are too embarrassed to ask! The third step should be directed toward a solution. If one is not apparent by this point in the conversation, a leader can invite suggestions.

> Dorothy, I feel that this job is very important to our work. It needs to be done so that others can continue with their efforts. What would you suggest? Can you still be involved? If so, let's find a way to provide you with some help. Tell me what you would like to do.

A leader's obligation is to support, equip, and help a lagging volunteer. It is not wise to ignore problems or pretend that absence from meetings or failure to carry out responsibility is acceptable; others may follow suit and assume that the negligent volunteer's behavior is quite all right, that it is acceptable to do nothing.

Delegating is an essential leadership tool. It broadens the base of participation and helps prevent leader burnout. Those who delegate responsibility will be most successful if they supervise, encourage, and require accountability.

18

RECORD KEEPING
AND EVALUATION

Records and evaluations encourage order.
Experiences of the past guide us as we minister in
the present and plan for the future.

Record keeping and evaluation are tedious jobs for most
people. As leaders, we sometimes neglect such paper-
work because it is time-consuming and may not be a
high priority in the light of other work. Record keeping
and evaluation, however, are important organizational
tasks for several reasons.

First of all, they facilitate smooth transitions between
leaders. Even if a new leader has previous experience,
written data can update him or her with information on
the preceding year's work. For instance, suppose you
are asked to chair the Board of Parish Education. You
may agree to serve, thinking that because you served on

a parish education committee in another congregation several years ago, you know what the job entails. Your experience may indeed enable you to feel confident, but even if you are familiar with the task in general, you may not know the history of this specific congregation. You would greatly benefit from information related to the finances, traditions, and activities of this particular congregation's Board of Parish Education.

In addition, records and evaluations provide information that can save time. Imagine that you joined a congregation three years ago. Last month you were elected chairperson of the Fellowship Board. Your first responsibility is to plan the annual congregational picnic. You attended the picnic two years ago but don't remember many details. Last year you were sick and could not go. Therefore, you ask the congregation's president for some help. Which scenario would you prefer?

> The president of the congregation tells you to do whatever you would like to do. He says new ideas are needed. You feel uneasy because you have no idea what expectations the congregation may have for this event. Is barbecue a tradition? Would potluck work instead? Do you have to plan games? Would a square dance be okay? Is fall an important traditional time for the picnic, or could it be held in the spring? Was there a charge for the dinner last year, or was there a freewill offering to defray expenses? Where did last year's team get chairs and tables? Questions abound.

OR

> The president hands you a report of last year's picnic. In it you find not only a complete record of food purchased and a detailed description of activities, but also a list of suggestions for improvement. Last year's chairperson wrote: "Our location at the Baywood Park is a good one, but those who are handicapped have a difficult time parking close to the table area; we should

arrange designated parking spots for them. People seem to prefer having the meal catered but enjoy bringing desserts of their own. The cakewalk was great, but we should have it later in the afternoon; it is a big drawing card at the picnic, and people stay longer if it is held toward the end of the day. We need a better microphone for the worship service; some could not hear. People should be asked to bring their own lawn chairs because the park benches get uncomfortable after a while. A mixer would be a good activity to begin with; people need help to get better acquainted."

You would probably prefer the second scenario. You would feel a sense of relief to have the detailed report and thoughtful evaluation prepared by last year's chairperson. This report provides information you could use as a beginning point for your own planning. You would not waste valuable time in confusion.

Records from previous years do not limit but rather free us from some of the more basic worries. If we have information about how an event was handled in the past, we can feel more confident about our planning. Knowing successes and failures helps us direct our energies toward details that need improvement. Thus, if certain aspects were highly successful, most likely we will want to repeat them. If other aspects were disappointing, we may want to be innovative and try a different approach. Most of us unquestionably would prefer to have notes from the past to guide planning.

TYPES OF RECORD KEEPING

MINUTES

Minutes are an appropriate means of recording business that is being transacted on an official basis by the governing body or by the congregation. These two groups frequently address expenditures of money or changes in programming; it is wise, therefore, to keep a formal and accurate record of what transpires. Usually a secretary is designated to keep track of all action taken during the course of the meeting. These minutes should be summaries highlighting main points; they should be simple, clear, and not overly detailed. Lengthy notes describing every word said are not necessary in most situations. Experiment with readable formats. Minutes should be reader-friendly!

Minutes can also be helpful in recording committee work. Again, the format and amount of detail included should be appropriate to the situation. Simplicity and clarity are useful guidelines.

REPORTS

Reports differ from minutes in several ways. Whereas minutes describe meetings, reports provide detailed information about activities or events. Minutes are taken during a meeting while action is unfolding; reports are prepared in advance of the meeting and presented to convey new information, to provide a progress update, to summarize a project or event at its completion, or to review a year's activity. Minutes are usually kept by a designated person, such as a secretary; reports may be done by the chairperson, a committee member, or an entire group.

Written summary reports are usually optional, and people seldom take time to prepare them. Such reports should be a routine part of leadership, however. They are invaluable aids for future planning. Summary reports describe a project, an event, or an entire year's activity.

• *Single events*—Summary reports of a single event or project should contain factual information, such as statistics related to finances, supplies, or attendance;

they document tasks involved and planning timetables. These specific facts inform us, help us minimize duplication and error, and help us anticipate problems so that we can take steps to prevent them from occurring. Reports should contain information about both outcome (what was done) and process (how it was done).

Reports may also include evaluative comments. Often the conversations of people attending an event indicate whether or not the event is successful. If the participants complain about certain features, we can jot down their remarks and consider them when we write our report. Our notes of their reactions, together with input from team members and our own opinions, will enable us to make suggestions for future improvements. A written report that contains both facts and evaluative comments becomes an excellent planning tool. It preserves for future chairpersons information that might otherwise be forgotten with the passage of time.

• *Annual activity*—Rather than focusing on a single event or project, a summary report may review the work of an entire year. Comprehensive reports are usually prepared by boards and teams for the governing body or for the congregation. An annual report includes the following factual information: goals, names of group members, financial information, and a list of the year's activities with a brief description of each.

Annual reports should also include evaluation. A subjective interpretation of events provides valuable insights about overall strengths and weaknesses of a ministry area. A starting point for evaluation is addressing the question *Did we accomplish our goals?* The next group of persons who assume responsibility for a particular ministry task will find such information valuable.

The following report is an example of how material can be presented in written form. This report was written after completion of an Easter sunrise service and breakfast sponsored by the youth of a congregation. It includes suggestions for the future.

REPORT

Name of project/event: Easter sunrise service and breakfast sponsored by youth

Task: To plan, publicize, and conduct the Easter sunrise service; to cook and serve a breakfast for the congregation after the service

Committee: Pastor Klein and Al Peterson (co-chairpersons) Marsha Anhelt, Lee Hong, and Joey Flider

TIMETABLE

February
• Planned the worship service (details attached)

March
• Began to publicize the event (3 bulletin announcements and 2 newsletter articles attached)
• Planned the breakfast (menu and work assignments attached)
• Reviewed plans for the service

April
• Made announcements in church
• Rehearsed the worship service
• Set up for worship on church patio (details attached)
• Met at church Saturday afternoon before Easter to set up for the breakfast (number of workers, time involved, and description of work done included)
• Met at church at 5:30 A.M. on Easter to cook breakfast

Number served: 110

Supplies purchased or borrowed: (itemized list of groceries and other supplies attached)

Total expenditures: $140
Total income: $203 from freewill offering
Surplus: The $63 remaining after bills were paid was deposited in the youth fund for scholarships to summer church camp.

Comments and suggestions:

1. It was difficult to manage hymnals in the wind. We should print the song lyrics in the programs.

2. Having greeters at the entrance to the patio would have provided a warm welcome.

3. This year we didn't have any instruments to accompany our singing. It was hard to get people started. Maybe someone could play a guitar for the service next year.

4. Our pancakes got cold. We need to figure out a way to keep them hot. Maybe we could heat the syrup.

5. Volunteers forgot to bring the table decorations, and we had to request last minute help from some of the mothers. We were putting decorations on the tables as people began to arrive. We should have decorated on Saturday.

6. We were disappointed by the attendance. More publicity might help—especially talks in church.

–2–

Note: Those who write such a report should always anticipate questions that future workers might have and include answers to those questions in the report. For example, future planners of this breakfast might want to know whether this year's planners discussed selling tickets instead of taking a freewill offering. Was advance sign-up a good indication of the number of people that actually came? How did this year's cooks decide how much food to prepare? Who decided how the extra income would be used? What would they have done if the offering had not covered expenditures? Did they have a plan for making up the deficit? Some of these details would have added strength to the report.

There is no set form or body of content for such a report because there is an infinite variety of activities in congregational life. Each one requires special information. The rule to follow is this: Include anything you might find helpful if you were to lead this activity for the first time.

Leader's Notebook

One of the most valuable tools for incoming leaders is a leader's notebook. Notice the word *notebook*—not a cardboard box filled with loose papers, not a file folder containing a jumble of documents, and not a few scribbled directions on a scrap of notebook paper. A leader's notebook should not be a random assemblage of information. It should be an orderly account of what has transpired. A leader's records should be complete, detailed, and always geared toward leaving tracks for successors. Such a paper trail will prove invaluable to those who follow in leadership positions.

A newcomer who is given a leader's notebook can gain instant familiarity with the new job in an evening's time. Last year's records can provide answers to his or her questions, allowing the newcomer to avoid being overly reliant on the previous chairperson for help. Records also provide assurance about what the job entails. If we have a reliable account of what our new job will require of us, we can look for ways to improve what has been done rather than spin our wheels trying to figure out basics. The leader who provides a clear, organized record for his or her successor offers a valuable gift.

Evaluation

When we evaluate, we assess the merits or shortcomings of a project, an annual event, or a year's work. We seek a subjective review of how those involved perceived their activity. An evaluation exposes weakness so that steps can be taken to avoid the same mistakes in the future. An evaluation also identifies achievement so that future workers can benefit from good suggestions. Although helpful suggestions and comments can be included with minutes and reports, sometimes it is important to emphasize evaluation by making it a separate process.

How should an evaluation be done? Whenever possible, leaders should invite co-workers to get together to share ideas. Usually leaders ask a series of questions designed to stimulate reflection and critical thinking. Co-workers respond with their opinions. If members of the group differ in their response, several attitudes may be noted on the evaluation form. If evaluations reflect a broad range of input, their value as tools for future planning is greater than if they are prepared by only one or two individuals.

EVALUATION OF AN EVENT

Event:

Committee members:

Names of persons completing the evaluation:

1. What aspects of the event were especially successful?

2. Should this event be repeated next year? If so, what changes would you recommend?

3. What was the main value of this event?

4. Was funding adequate? If not, why not? Do you have any suggestions for gaining additional funding?

5. Did you have enough workers? If not, how many more are needed?

6. What suggestions do you have for the future?

7. Are there any resource people who could be contacted in the future? List their names and describe the kind of help they could provide.

The work of each major board should be evaluated annually. People tend to repeat patterns year after year unless evaluation occurs. Questions such as those on the following evaluation can guide discussion.

ANNUAL EVALUATION

Name of board:
Members:

Names of persons completing the evaluation:

Board goals:

1. Did we accomplish our goals this year? If not, why not?

2. What were our primary accomplishments? Why were these efforts especially successful?

3. What were our main frustrations? Why?

4. Was our funding adequate?

5. Are there any ways we could cooperate with other boards in the future?

6. What suggestions could be made for next year's board?

7. Did we have sufficient support, helpers, and participants for our activities?

8. What goals should we consider in the future?

At some point a pastor and representatives from the governing body can meet with each board chairperson to review the work being done. The chairperson can bring a copy of the evaluation prepared by his or her group to help review the year's activity. The specific purpose of the conference is to examine all aspects of a particular program or ministry.

Conferences between board chairpersons and members of the governing body have important benefits. First of all, chairpersons feel encouraged when the pastor or other leaders show interest in their efforts. Second, the conference provides a setting in which to talk about problems. Third, it provides a context for creative thinking and exploration of new ideas. Finally, the conference gives members of the governing body an opportunity to become informed about details of ministry that may have escaped their attention. These conference times not only provide forums for evaluation, but they allow opportunity for leaders to advise, encourage, and support those who counsel with them.

Records inform, guide, and help train future leaders for ministry. Carefully kept written accounts demonstrate the importance we attach to our work. Both factual records and evaluation help us upgrade the quality of our future endeavors. They reveal our awareness that history teaches valuable lessons!

WHERE SHOULD YOU BEGIN?

Whether you are a pastor or a layperson, your head may be full of ideas at this point. You want to get started, but where should you begin? Like the child surveying the bobbing apples, you don't want to randomly bob here and there and end up with only a wet face! How should you choose an apple—a place to begin?

The place to begin is goal setting. The governing body should allow three months for establishing a vision statement and a congregational annual goal. A sense of direction is the highest priority. While deliberation on goal setting is in progress, chairpersons at all levels can simultaneously work on developing effective agendas and thereby streamline their meetings; innovation and better use of time will energize and excite group members. The first quarter, therefore, should be used by leaders to write both a vision statement and an annual congregational goal. At the same time, leaders can seek to improve agendas for all meetings.

During the second quarter, leaders can begin to focus on leadership skills and board goals. Leadership skills can be addressed in a retreat, a Saturday seminar, or several evening meetings of congregational leaders and board chairpersons. These can be interactive sessions that mix information with small group sharing and role-playing.

Leaders can devote the last six months of the year to simplifying structures. This involves listing all existing organizations, assessing their value, and grouping them into a small number of major categories. Once a simple, clear structure is in place and a vision statement accepted, leaders in successive years will not have to repeat those tasks. Structure can be reevaluated every three to five years, but massive change probably will not be necessary. Therefore, after the first year, annual focus will be directed only in two directions: formation of goals and leadership training.

Consider the hours spent in meetings. Isn't it time to fill those hours with maximum productivity? One person's enthusiasm can revolutionize a group. *You* can help your congregation experience new life. The goal is to establish committees that facilitate mission and do not bog down in outmoded patterns.

Do you wish for dynamic, effective ministry? Why wait? *Develop a winning parish team now!*

To Order Copies

If unavailable in local bookstores, LangMarc
Publishing will fill your order within 24 hours.
Postal Orders: LangMarc Publishing • P.O. 33817 •
San Antonio, Texas 78265-3817

Bobbing for Apples—With Success!
$11.95

Quantity Discounts: 10% discount for 3-4 books; 15%
for 5-9; 20% for 10 or more copies.

Add Shipping: Book rate $1.50 for 1; 50 cents for each
additional book. $3.00 for priority mail 1-2 books. Call
for less costly UPS charges on quantity orders.

1-800-864-1648 • Fax: 210-822-5014

Please send payment with order:

——— Books at $11.95　　　　　　　————————
　　　Less quantity discount　　　————————
　　　Total for books　　　　　　————————
　　　Sales tax (TX only)　　　　————————
　　　Shipping　　　　　　　　　————————
　　　Check enclosed:　　　　　　————————

Send to:

——————————————————————————————
——————————————————————————————
——————————————————————————————

Phone: